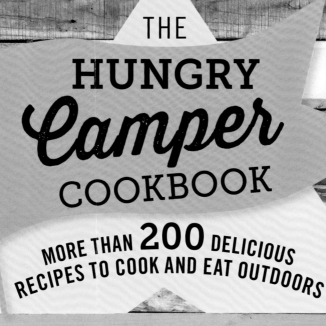

THE
HUNGRY
Camper
COOKBOOK

MORE THAN 200 DELICIOUS
RECIPES TO COOK AND EAT OUTDOORS

spruce

An Hachette UK Company
www.hachette.co.uk

First published in Great Britain in 2015 by
Spruce, a division of Octopus Publishing Group Ltd
Endeavour House, 189 Shaftesbury Avenue
London WC2H 8JY
www.octopusbooksusa.com

Distributed in the US by Hachette Book Group
1290 Avenue of the Americas
4th and 5th Floors, New York, NY 10020
Distributed in Canada by Canadian Manda Group
664 Annette Street, Toronto
Ontario, Canada M6S 2C8

ISBN 978-1-84601-496-3
Printed and bound in China
10 9 8 7 6 5 4 3 2 1

Cooking times given for the recipes in this book
should be used as only a guide—always check food
is cooked through and piping hot before eating. The
juices of poultry should run clear when the thickest
part is pierced with a sharp knife.

Contents

Introduction

No one can forget the excitement of their first camping vacation. The passing of years tends to add a romantic slant to the whole experience, with campfires, toasted marshmallows, and nature walks helping to erase memories of soggy sleeping bags, torrential rain, and numb toes. There's no denying the thrill of a camping trip—from the planning and packing to choosing a pitch, setting up camp, and cooking food over an open fire.

Camping provides a rare chance to connect with your inner child, reigniting the adventurous spirit that has been worn down by the daily grind. And kids thrive on the freedom and adventure of a vacation where the normal routine is tossed aside and no one nags them about personal hygiene. It's also a great opportunity to give them some responsibility, which will be richly rewarded by the freedom they'll enjoy.

If you're going to fully embrace the camping experience, it's best to leave the modern world at home as far as possible. It's difficult to bond with nature if you're trying to get a Wi-Fi connection to pick up work e-mails, or you cut short the campfire banter to go inside and watch TV. Camping is all about removing yourself from the frenetic pace of everyday life and taking a step back to basics. It's about having a conversation over dinner instead of sitting in silence on the couch; it's about teaching your kids that nature can compete with smartphones and tablets on the entertainment front. And, of course, it wouldn't be a true camping experience without spending at least one entire day inside watching the rain pour down.

WHAT TO PACK

When you pack for a camping trip, every scrap of space is at a premium, which is why you need to be methodical—perhaps verging on the obsessive—about making lists and getting organized well in advance of departure day. Unless you have all your camping equipment and supplies constantly packed up and ready to go at a moment's notice, you'll need to begin preparations a week or so beforehand. The last thing you want to do on vacation is spend hours trekking around out-of-town shopping malls searching for vital pieces of equipment that you forgot to pack.

The exact contents of your car will be dictated by the type of camping "camp" you fall into: purists will take the bare minimum and will be happy to survive on canned food and one change of clothes; "glampers" will need a few more luxury items in order to enjoy the experience; and those traveling with kids will be lucky to get away with an inch of free space remaining in the car or van.

TENT

If you're camping under cloth, your tent and sleeping equipment will obviously be the big priorities and will also take up the most amount of space. As a general rule of thumb, the bigger the tent, the more chances there will be that everyone is still on speaking terms at the end of the vacation. If you can afford to, buy a tent with separate sleeping and living areas and enough space to stand up straight and move around—it might not seem such a big deal during a heat wave, but you'll appreciate the extra space when that freak thunderstorm unleashes itself over the site.

BEDDING

If you love the idea of camping but also love the idea of getting some sleep while you're on vacation, it's definitely worth considering inflatable mattresses or air beds. Sleeping mats have their place but that's usually on survival expeditions. There's no shame in packing a few home comforts and your joints will thank you for it in the morning. If you have space, bring plenty of blankets and pillows as well: it can get cold in a tent at night. If you think about it logically, the only thing separating you from the elements is a sliver of man-made fiber—why on earth wouldn't you bring a few extra sleeping layers? You'll have the last laugh when the temperature plummets and you're snuggled up in your sleeping bag and blankets.

LIVING & SLEEPING CHECKLIST

- ☐ Tent, tent pegs, and mallet
- ☐ Groundsheets
- ☐ Sleeping bags
- ☐ Pillows
- ☐ Air bed and pump or sleeping mats
- ☐ Fold-up table and chairs
- ☐ Rugs and blankets (for chilly evenings)
- ☐ Towels
- ☐ Wet weather gear
- ☐ Extra socks
- ☐ Flip-flops (for bathroom trips)
- ☐ Rain boots and hiking boots

FIRST AID

You can pretty much guarantee that someone will get a cut, bite, headache, or stubbed toe within minutes of your arrival, so a well-stocked first aid kit is essential. If you've used it before, always check it before you pack and replace anything that has run low or reached an expiration date. Keep the kit somewhere easy to access and make sure everyone knows where it is so there's no fumbling around late at the night.

KEEPING CLEAN

The camper's code accepts that grooming standards can be lowered—waiting in line for a shower that wouldn't be out of place in a penal colony is a surefire way for personal hygiene to take a nose dive. It's a little like eating garlic: If everyone becomes a soap dodger, no one will notice the smell. But, there should be a token nod toward grooming and you should at least pack towels, shower gel, shampoo, and toothpaste. And it goes without saying that you can never have enough toilet paper.

FIRST AID & TOILETRIES CHECKLIST

- ☐ Toothbrushes and toothpaste
- ☐ Razor and shaving cream
- ☐ Shower gel
- ☐ Shampoo
- ☐ Deodorant
- ☐ Toilet paper
- ☐ Hairbrush and hairbands
- ☐ Nail scissors and tweezers
- ☐ Sunscreen lotion
- ☐ Insect repellent
- ☐ Antihistamine
- ☐ Thermometer
- ☐ Antiseptic cream
- ☐ Bandages
- ☐ Pain-killers
- ☐ Prescription medication

OTHER USEFUL EQUIPMENT

- ☐ Camera
- ☐ Cell phone charger
- ☐ Clock radio
- ☐ Travel clothesline and pegs
- ☐ Multitool and penknife
- ☐ Flashlight
- ☐ Maps and compass
- ☐ Sewing kit
- ☐ String
- ☐ Travel wash
- ☐ Umbrella
- ☐ Duct tape
- ☐ Disposable wipes
- ☐ Ear plugs (for next-door snorers!)
- ☐ Coins (for showers or lockers)
- ☐ Toys and games

COOKING EQUIPMENT

The amount of equipment you bring depends on whether you intend mealtimes to be a central focus or just a chance to refuel. You will need a decent double-burner camping stove at the least, with plenty of extra fuel to see you through the trip. If you're planning on embracing the romance of alfresco dining and cooking on a campfire, you should bring fuel (wood or barbecue coals). It's worth checking in advance if the campsite allows open fires and sells fuel, because this may be something less to carry.

A lot of camping recipes are designed for cooking in one pot, so make sure you bring one large enough for the whole party. A skillet is also essential for morning fried breakfasts. Bring enough dishes and cutlery for everyone to eat together without playing "pass the fork," and don't forget wine glasses—unless you want to tip the coffee dregs out of a mug when evening approaches.

COOLERS

If you don't have a camping refrigerator, you will need to take at least one cooler with you. As a rule, ground meat, poultry, and fish shouldn't be kept for more than two days, but steaks and chops will keep for three to four, and eggs, bacon, and dairy products should keep in sealed containers for up to a week. Some campsites have freezers available so you can refreeze your ice packs, so mark them with your name.

When packing your cooler, use every ounce of space, fill any gaps with bubble wrap, and try not to open it too often. If possible, keep food and drinks in separate coolers. This is especially important for any meat that you're taking with you; if you keep frozen meat undisturbed in a tightly sealed cooler, it will keep fresher for longer.

COOKING EQUIPMENT CHECKLIST

- ☐ Double-burner camping stove and/or barbecue grill
- ☐ Grill rack, charcoal, wood, and newspaper for barbecue and/or campfire
- ☐ Lighter or matches
- ☐ Barbecue tongs and metal skewers
- ☐ Large and small heavy cooking saucepans with lids
- ☐ Large nonstick, lidded skillet
- ☐ Ridged grill pan (if using a stove)
- ☐ Meat thermometer
- ☐ Kitchen knife and cutting board
- ☐ Cheese grater
- ☐ Plastic mixing bowl, measuring cups, spoons, and colander
- ☐ Pastry brush
- ☐ Rolling pin; not essential, but useful for crushing seeds and rolling pizza dough
- ☐ Can and bottle openers
- ☐ Wooden spoon, spatula, and slotted spoon
- ☐ Vegetable peeler
- ☐ Mess kits with plates, bowls, and cutlery
- ☐ Paper towels and garbage bags
- ☐ Foil, plastic wrap, and freezer bags
- ☐ Plastic containers with lids
- ☐ Cooler(s) and ice packs
- ☐ Dish-washing bowl and liquid
- ☐ Dish towels and oven mitts

FOOD ESSENTIALS CHECKLIST

- ☐ Vegetable oil and olive oil, for cooking
- ☐ Butter or spread
- ☐ Salt and pepper
- ☐ Tea bags, coffee, and sugar
- ☐ Condiments
- ☐ Eggs
- ☐ Cans of beans, tomatoes, fruit
- ☐ Bread
- ☐ Milk
- ☐ Soft drinks
- ☐ Alcohol
- ☐ Onions and garlic
- ☐ Pasta, rice, noodles
- ☐ Potato chips and other snacks

COOKING METHODS
& Techniques

CAMPFIRE COOKING

If your cozy campfire is also your oven, you need to treat it a little differently; instead of continuously stoking up the logs, you need to let the flames burn down into charcoal so the temperature is white hot and even—and perfect for cooking. Alternatively, you can move the cooking coals over to one side and stoke up the flames on the other. Now you can use a simple campfire grill rack to cook your food directly over the coals.

Alternatively, you can wrap potatoes, fish, and meat in sheets of heavy-duty aluminum foil—adding some oil, herbs, or other flavorings—and place these directly in the coals. Because heat in a campfire is never completely even, make sure you rotate the packages occasionally so that they cook evenly.

BARBECUE

Some campsites provide designated barbecue areas and you might have a traditional charcoal variety or a gas option. If you're cooking for a large group of people or are preparing a number of dishes, a barbecue might be a better option than the campfire. With charcoal grills, the same rules apply as campfire cooking, in that you will need to spark up the coals at least 30 minutes before you plan to start cooking.

CAMPING STOVE

If you need some instant power for a quick plate of egg and beans, a double-burner camping stove offers a convenient way to cook and can also be combined with cooking over coals to get the best of both worlds. It goes without saying that you should make sure you bring enough gas to last the duration of your trip, and test the stove before you leave home to make sure it's in good working order, especially if you haven't used it for a while.

A NOTE ON FOOD SAFETY

It takes a little practice to master the art of cooking by fire and flashlight. If you want to remain friends with your camping companions, it's imperative to be sure food is completely cooked through before you serve it. Campfires and barbecues have a fairly relaxed temperament when it comes to maintaining temperature, so although chicken breasts may have been grilling for hours and are charred on the outside, that's no guarantee that they're cooked in the middle. Cooking times given for the recipes in this book should be used as only a guide; always check food is cooked through and piping hot before you start eating. You could include a meat thermometer to be sure that barbecued meat is cooked through, or cut into chicken to test it for clear juices.

Perfect Pitch

There are various schools of thought when it comes to choosing the perfect place on the campsite to pitch your tent or park up your recreation vehicle, but, while the highest spot in the site might be one camper's idea of the ultimate prize, it is just as probable that it's another's exposed wind tunnel of hell. Once you've become a more seasoned camper, you'll probably have your pitch-picking skills honed to perfection, having tried and tested a number of different areas on different sites.

The weather will always be a major factor when choosing your location, which is why the general thinking is that a flat, raised pitch will see you through the worst that a stormy night can throw at you. However, add a gusty wind into the mix and a pitch perched on raised ground might not be the ideal choice; you'll spend a sleepless night wondering how firm your mallet arm was when you knocked in the tent pegs. Here are a few other factors to consider before staking your claim on a spot.

Shelter—this is especially important if you plan on trying to light an open fire for cooking.

Position—try to set the tent so that the sleeping area faces the setting sun, otherwise you'll be in for an early wake-up call when the sun rises.

Space—if the prime spot is also the smallest, look around for somewhere else. You need some space around your tent or vehicle for cooking, seating, hanging up clothes, etc.

Neighbors—this is down to personal preference. If you like to talk with other campers over your morning cup of coffee, set yourself up in a middle pitch; if you want to be at one with nature, then search out a more isolated spot.

Families—if you have children, it makes sense to pick a pitch near other families; the kids should make friends, giving you some much-needed downtime. Plus, if your children have a meltdown, you'll get sympathy instead of dirty looks.

Call of nature—pitching up next to the lavatories isn't everyone's idea of the perfect wilderness weekend, but if your bladder can't make it through the night, you might want to keep the conveniences close by.

PREPARE & COOK AHEAD

It's great to prepare big family meals on camping trips, but be realistic about what's achievable when you're preparing dinner in the dark on a small gas stove or over a wood fire. You can save yourself a great deal of time, effort, and angst by preparing a few essentials at home. It's not cheating; think of it more as preemptive stress relief.

MEASURING

Get organized in advance of your trip and make a meal plan. Measure all the dry ingredients you'll need and put into sealable plastic freezer bags so you carry only what you need. To avoid taking a mortar and pestle, crush any seeds or pods required at home, then transfer to small, lidded containers.

GRATED CHEESE

If you grate and store it in an airtight container, you can also dispense with a grater (although a small one is always useful for recipes requiring citrus zest, grated ginger, or veg).

BREAD CRUMBS

If you're making burgers, it is useful to make fresh bread crumbs in advance and store them in a sealable plastic freezer bag. Alternatively, make the complete patties in advance and store in an airtight container in a cooler for up to 1 day.

MARINATE

To add extra flavor to meat or fish, marinate it overnight before you set off, then you can arrive, crank up the campfire, and have a delicious, flavorsome meal.

PASTA

Cook the pasta of your choice in a large saucepan of lightly salted boiling water according to package directions until just tender, drain well, return to the pan, and stir through a little olive oil to stop it from sticking. Let cool, then store in sealable bags. It can be quickly reheated or stirred into a sauce when you're at the campsite.

BAKED POTATOES

These can be cooked in advance, then wrapped in aluminum foil and put onto the campfire for an authentic alfresco snack.

BOILED EGGS

Perfect for salads, sandwiches, and snacks, cook and cool the eggs before you leave.

SAUCES

A container full of prepared curry or pasta sauce will provide a quick and delicious camping meal. Stir in some vegetables or meat and serve with cooked pasta or rice for the first night.

MEAT

Cooked meat can be kept chilled in a cooler for a day and then completely reheated for a quick dinner—try chicken pieces for an alfresco curry or barbecue skewers; pulled pork to serve in wraps, burger buns, or baguettes; and drumsticks for a fireside buffet.

MAKE A MEAL OF IT

Prepared one-dish meals, such as chili, stew, casseroles, and ratatouille, are ideal for camping. You can make batches and keep them frozen in sealed containers in your cooler for up to 2 days.

BASIC RECIPES

Making a few homemade essentials to take with you ensures you always have the makings of a tasty meal on hand.

Granola

1 cup mixed nuts
spray olive oil, for greasing
2 cups rolled oats
1 tablespoon maple syrup

Makes 4 servings
Prep time 5 minutes, plus cooling
Cooking time 15 minutes

1   Preheat the oven to 350°F. Heat the nuts in a dry skillet over medium-low heat for 3-4 minutes, shaking the pan occasionally, until toasted. Let cool, then coarsely chop.

2   Spray a baking sheet lightly with spray oil. Put the oats and nuts in a bowl and stir in the maple syrup. Spread the mixture out on the prepared baking sheet and bake in the preheated oven for 5 minutes.

3   Remove from the oven and stir well. Return to the oven and bake for another 3-4 minutes, until lightly toasted. Let cool, then store in an airtight container for up to 1 week.

Hot Harissa Sauce

1 tablespoon coriander seeds
1 teaspoon caraway seeds
3 tablespoons olive oil
1 red bell pepper, cored, seeded, and coarsely chopped
1 small red onion, coarsely chopped
1 red chile, seeded and chopped
3 garlic cloves, chopped
1/4 cup fresh cilantro leaves, torn into pieces
1/2 teaspoon celery salt
2/3 tomato puree or tomato sauce

Serves 4-6
Prep time 10 minutes
Cooking time 5 minutes

1   Using a mortar and pestle, grind the coriander and caraway seeds until lightly crushed. Alternatively, use a small bowl and the end of a rolling pin.

2   Transfer the seeds to a skillet, add the oil, red bell pepper, and onion and cook over low heat for 5 minutes, or until the vegetables are soft.

3   Transfer the mixture to a food processor or blender and add the chile, garlic, cilantro, celery salt, and tomato puree or sauce.

4   Blend until smooth, scraping the mixture down from the sides of the bowl, if necessary. Let cool, then transfer to an airtight container and store in a cooler for up to 2 days.

Homemade Cookies

1 1/2 cups rolled oats
1 1/4 cups all-purpose flour, plus extra for dusting
1/4 lb plus 2 tablespoons (1 1/4 sticks) salted butter, cut into small pieces, plus extra for greasing
1/3 cup firmly packed light brown sugar

Makes about 20 cookies
Prep time 10 minutes, plus chilling
Cooking time 15 minutes

1   Put the oats and flour into a food processor, add the butter, and blend until the mixture resembles coarse bread crumbs. Add the sugar and mix to a dough. Wrap in plastic wrap and chill for 30 minutes.

2   Preheat the oven to 375°F and grease 2 baking sheets. Roll out the dough on a floured work surface to 1/8 inch thick and cut out 3-inch disks with a cookie cutter. Transfer to the baking sheets, spaced slightly apart, and bake in the oven for about 15 minutes, until pale golden.

3   Transfer to a wire rack and let cool. Store in an airtight container for up to 1 week. These can also be used to make S'mores on page 243.

BACON & MAPLE SYRUP PANCAKES

MOLASSES & MUSTARD BEANS

POTATO DROP PANCAKES

CRÊPES WITH BLUEBERRIES

BREAKFASTS

14 HERB OMELET WITH MUSTARD MUSHROOMS

15 SMOKED SALMON SCRAMBLED EGGS

16 TRAFFIC LIGHT SCRAMBLED EGGS

17 MUSHROOM CRÊPES

18 CREAMY MUSHROOMS ON TOAST

19 BACON & MAPLE SYRUP PANCAKES

20 CRÊPES WITH BLUEBERRIES

22 BUTTERMILK PANCAKES

23 BANANA & CARDAMOM PANCAKES

24 FRENCH TOASTS WITH BANANAS, PECANS, & CARAMEL

25 ORANGE FRENCH TOAST

26 POTATO DROP PANCAKES

27 MOLASSES & MUSTARD BEANS

30 BOSTON BAKED BEANS

31 RUSTIC PARMESAN & OLIVE BREAD

32 SUMMER BERRY GRANOLA

32 QUINOA & GOLDEN RAISIN PORRIDGE

33 BANANA & CINNAMON OATMEAL

34 CORNED BEEF HASH

35 SAUSAGE & BACON BURGERS

36 POACHED EGGS, BACON, & MUFFINS

BANANA & CINNAMON OATMEAL

Herb Omelet
WITH MUSTARD MUSHROOMS

IF YOU PREFER, COOK HALF THE EGG MIXTURE AT A TIME TO MAKE TWO SMALLER OMELETS.

1 Beat together the mustard and butter in a bowl, then spread over the undersides of the mushrooms. Put them, mustard side up, on an aluminum foil-lined grill rack over a barbecue grill or campfire, or in a hot ridged grill pan, and cook for about 5 minutes or until tender.

2 Meanwhile, beat together the herbs and eggs in a bowl, then season with salt and black pepper.

3 Melt a pat of butter in a skillet until foaming, then swirl in the egg mixture and cook over medium heat until just set. Carefully slide the omelet onto a plate, add the mushrooms, and serve.

1 tablespoon whole-grain mustard
3 tablespoons butter, softened, plus extra for frying
4 flat mushrooms
2 tablespoons chopped mixed fresh herbs (such as chives, parsley, and tarragon)
4 eggs
salt and black pepper

Serves **2**
Prep time **5 minutes**
Cooking time **10 minutes**

CAMPING TIP

Keep your toothbrushes fresh and clean (and stop them from wetting the rest of your toiletries once they have been used) by loosely wrapping them individually in aluminum foil after each use.

SMOKED SALMON
Scrambled Eggs

3 extra-large eggs
1 tablespoon milk
a pat of butter, plus extra for
   spreading (optional)
1-2 slices of whole wheat bread
1 tablespoon light cream (optional)
1-1½ oz smoked salmon, cut into
   narrow strips
1 teaspoon finely snipped chives
salt and black pepper

Serves **1**
Prep time **10 minutes**
Cooking time **about 5 minutes**

1 Beat the eggs in a bowl with a fork. Add the milk and season with salt and black pepper.

2 Melt the butter in a skillet over low heat until foaming. Pour the eggs into the foaming butter and cook, stirring constantly and scraping the bottom of the pan and bringing the eggs from the outside to the center. The eggs are done when they form soft, creamy curds and are barely set.

3 Meanwhile, toast the bread in a ridged grill pan or on a grill rack over a barbecue grill or campfire. Spread with butter, if desired.

4 Remove the eggs from the heat and stir in the cream, if using, the salmon, and chives. Pile onto the hot toast and serve immediately.

TRAFFIC LIGHT
SCRAMBLED EGGS

3 tablespoons olive oil
1 small onion, finely chopped
½ green bell pepper, cored,
   seeded, and coarsely chopped
½ red bell pepper, cored, seeded,
   and coarsely chopped
½ yellow bell pepper, cored,
   seeded, and coarsely chopped
1 garlic clove, crushed
6 eggs, beaten
½ cup light cream or milk
4 thick slices of whole wheat
   bread

Serves **4**
Prep time **10 minutes**
Cooking time **10-15 minutes**

1 Heat the oil in a skillet, add the onion and bell peppers, and cook over medium heat for about 5 minutes, until softened. Add the garlic and cook for another 1 minute, then add 3 tablespoons of water. Cover with a lid or aluminum foil and simmer for 2 minutes.

2 Beat together the eggs and cream or milk in a bowl. Remove the lid or foil from the pan, pour in the eggs, and stir over low heat with a wooden spoon until the eggs are creamy and just set.

3 Meanwhile, toast the bread in a ridged grill pan or on a grill rack over a barbecue grill or campfire. Serve the eggs spooned over the warm toast.

MUSHROOM CRÊPES

1 Put the flour, milk, egg, and salt and black pepper into a bowl and beat until smooth. Set aside.

2 To make the filling, put all the ingredients into a small saucepan and cook over medium-low heat for 5–10 minutes, stirring occasionally, until the mushrooms are softened.

3 Heat a little oil in a skillet over medium heat. Pour in a ladleful of the batter and cook for about 1 minute, or until golden underneath. Carefully flip the crêpe over and cook on the other side. Slide onto a plate, add one-quarter of the mushroom filling, roll up, and serve.

4 Repeat with the remaining batter and filling to make another 3 crêpes, adding a little more oil to the pan as required.

⅓ cup all-purpose flour
⅔ cup milk
1 medium egg, beaten
olive oil
salt and black pepper

Filling
4 cups chopped cremini mushrooms
1 bunch of scallions, finely chopped
1 garlic clove, chopped
1 (14½ oz) can diced tomatoes, drained
2 tablespoons chopped oregano

Serves **4**
Prep time **10 minutes**
Cooking time **20 minutes**

CAMPING TIP

Packing up the car can take a long time, so try to get as much organized the night before as possible. You should aim to arrive at the campsite early so you have a choice of pitches and a stress-free setup.

CREAMY
MUSHROOMS
ON TOAST

1 tablespoon olive oil
1 tablespoon lime juice
1 small onion, chopped
8 mushrooms, sliced
1 tablespoon light soy sauce
2 tablespoons ricotta cheese
4 slices of whole wheat bread

Serves **2**
Prep time **5 minutes**
Cooking time **10 minutes**

1 Heat the oil in a skillet, add the lime juice, and sauté the onion and mushrooms over medium heat for about 5 minutes, until softened. Stir in the soy sauce and ricotta.

2 Meanwhile, toast the bread in a ridged grill pan or on a grill rack over a barbecue grill or campfire.

3 Pour the mushrooms on top of the toast and serve immediately.

BACON *& Maple Syrup* PANCAKES

2¹⁄₃ cups all-purpose flour
2¹⁄₂ teaspoons baking powder
¹⁄₂ teaspoon salt
1 egg, lightly beaten
1³⁄₄ cups milk
2 tablespoons butter, melted
olive oil
8 smoked bacon slices
maple syrup, to serve

Serves **4**
Prep time **5 minutes**
Cooking time **15–30 minutes**

1 Put the flour, baking powder, and salt into a bowl. Make a well in the center and gradually beat in the egg and milk until smooth. Stir in the melted butter.

2 Heat a little oil in a skillet over medium heat. Pour in about ¹⁄₂ cup of the batter and cook for 1–2 minutes, or until bubbles start appearing on the surface. Carefully flip the pancake over and cook for another 1–2 minutes on the other side until golden. Slide onto a plate, cover with aluminum foil, and keep warm. Repeat with the remaining batter to make another 7 pancakes, adding a little more oil to the pan as required.

3 Meanwhile, heat a ridged grill pan over medium-high heat, add the bacon, and cook for about 2 minutes on each side until golden and cooked through.

4 Serve the pancakes topped with the bacon and drizzled with maple syrup.

CRÊPES
WITH **BLUEBERRIES**

1 cup all-purpose flour
1 egg
1¼ cups milk
2 cups blueberries
2 tablespoons fresh orange juice
1–2 tablespoons sugar, to taste
vegetable oil
¼ cup crème fraîche or Greek
  yogurt, to serve (optional)

Serves **4**
Prep time **5 minutes**
Cooking time **30 minutes**

1 Put the flour, egg, and milk into a bowl and beat until smooth. Set aside.

2 Put the blueberries, orange juice, and sugar into a small saucepan over low heat and warm gently until the blueberries begin to burst. Remove from the heat and let cool slightly.

3 Heat a little oil in a skillet over medium heat. Pour in a little of the batter, swirl to coat thinly, and cook gently for 2 minutes, or until golden underneath. Carefully flip the crêpe over and cook on the other side. Slide onto a plate, cover with aluminum foil, and keep warm. Repeat with the remaining batter to make another 7 crêpes, adding a little more oil to the pan as required.

4 Serve the crêpes with the warm blueberries and dollops of crème fraîche or Greek yogurt, if desired.

CAMPING TIP

Check out the facilities on your campsite before your trip. An on-site store will be handy for essential groceries, while rules regarding fires and barbecues will have a big impact on what you bring and your meal planning.

BUTTERMILK
Pancakes

LIGHT, FLUFFY, AND DELICIOUS, THESE PANCAKES ARE BEST SERVED STRAIGHT FROM THE PAN—TRY TOPPING WITH A LITTLE BUTTER AND PRESERVES. IF YOU PREFER TO SERVE ALL THE PANCAKES TOGETHER, KEEP THEM HOT ON A PLATE COVERED WITH ALUMINUM FOIL WHILE YOU COOK THE REMAINING BATTER. IF YOU DON'T HAVE ANY BUTTERMILK, USE LOW-FAT PLAIN YOGURT MIXED WITH HALF THE AMOUNT OF MILK INSTEAD.

1 Put the flour, baking powder, and baking soda into a bowl and make a well in the center. Put the egg whites into a separate clean bowl and beat until they form soft peaks.

2 Add the egg yolks and buttermilk to the flour mixture and beat until smooth. With a large spoon, fold in the egg whites.

3 Heat a little oil in a skillet over medium heat. Drop large spoonfuls of the batter into the pan, spacing them slightly apart, and cook for about 3 minutes or until the undersides are golden and the tops are bubbling. Flip the pancakes over and cook on the other side until cooked through. Remove from the pan and serve warm with butter and preserves.

4 Repeat with the remaining batter, adding a little more oil to the pan as required.

1⅔ cups all-purpose flour
1 teaspoon baking powder
½ teaspoon baking soda
2 eggs, separated
1 cup plus 2 tablespoons buttermilk
vegetable oil

To serve
butter
preserves

Serves **4**
Prep time **15 minutes**
Cooking time **20 minutes**

COOKING TIP

For the second batch, wipe the pan with a piece of folded paper towel moistened with a little oil before adding the batter.

BANANA & CARDAMOM
PANCAKES

BANANA AND CARDAMOM ARE AN UNBEATABLE COMBINATION, SO IF YOU'RE TAKING A LOT OF RIPE BANANAS ON YOUR CAMPING TRIP, THIS IS FOR YOU!

1 Mash the bananas in a large bowl, add the flour, sugar, melted butter, milk, and egg, and beat until smooth. Stir in the cardamom.

2 Heat a little oil in a skillet over medium heat. Drop 3-4 tablespoons of the batter into the pan, spacing them slightly apart, and cook for 2-3 minutes. Flip the pancakes over and cook on the other side for another 2 minutes, or until lightly browned and cooked through. Remove from the pan and serve warm with honey.

3 Repeat with the remaining batter, adding a little more oil to the pan as required.

4 ripe bananas
2½ cups all-purpose flour
2½ teaspoons baking powder
2 tablespoons sugar
2 tablespoons melted butter
½ cup milk
1 egg, lightly beaten
2 teaspoons crushed cardamom seeds
vegetable oil, for frying
honey, to serve

Serves **4**
Prep time **10 minutes**
Cooking time **10-15 minutes**

FRENCH TOASTS

WITH BANANAS, PECANS, & CARAMEL

1 egg
1 tablespoon sugar
3 tablespoons milk
1/4 teaspoon ground cinnamon
2 thick slices of white or whole-
  grain bread, crusts removed,
  if desired
2 tablespoons unsalted butter
1 teaspoon vegetable oil
2 tablespoons coarsely
  chopped pecans
1/4 cup caramel sauce
  (dulce de leche)
2 small bananas

Serves **2**
Prep time **10 minutes**
Cooking time **15-20 minutes**

1 Beat the egg in a shallow dish, adding the sugar, milk, and cinnamon once the egg is broken up. Dip the bread slices into the mixture, turning them over so they've absorbed the batter on both sides.

2 Heat the butter and oil in a skillet until foaming. Add the bread slices and cook, turning once, until golden on both sides. Transfer to plates.

3 Drain off any oil in the pan and add the pecans. Cook until lightly toasted, shaking the pan frequently. Add the caramel sauce, then the bananas, slicing them into the caramel.

4 Stir for a few minutes to heat through. Spoon the sauce onto the toast and serve.

ORANGE
French Toast

2 oranges
6 slices of raisin bread
2 eggs
¼ cup milk
¼ teaspoon ground cinnamon
2 tablespoons butter
2 tablespoons vegetable oil
sour cream or Greek yogurt,
  to serve (optional)

Serves **4**
Prep time **10 minutes**
Cooking time **10 minutes**

1 Pare the zest from one of the oranges with a lemon zester or sharp knife and set aside. Using a sharp knife, remove the peel and pith from both oranges, then cut between the membranes to separate the segments and set aside.

2 Cut the bread slices in half diagonally. Beat together the eggs, milk, and cinnamon in a shallow dish.

3 Heat half the butter and oil in a skillet until foaming. Quickly dip half the bread triangles into the egg mixture, turning them over so they've absorbed the batter on both sides, then add to the pan. Cook for about 5 minutes, turning once, until golden on both sides. Remove from the pan, cover with aluminum foil, and keep warm. Repeat with the remaining butter, oil, and bread.

4 Top the toast with the orange segments and zest, and serve with dollops of sour cream or yogurt, if desired.

Potato
DROP PANCAKES

1 Cook the potatoes in a saucepan of lightly salted boiling water for about 15 minutes, or until completely tender. Drain well, return to the saucepan, and mash until smooth. Let cool slightly.

2 Beat in the baking powder, then the eggs, milk, and a little salt and black pepper, and continue to beat until everything is evenly combined.

3 Heat a little oil in a skillet over medium heat. Drop heaping spoonfuls of the mixture into the pan, spacing them slightly apart, and sauté for about 5 minutes, turning once, until golden on both sides. Remove from the pan and serve warm with grilled bacon and tomatoes, if desired.

4 Repeat with the remaining potato mixture to make 12 drop pancakes, adding a little more oil to the pan as required.

5 large russet potatoes, peeled
    and cut into small chunks
1½ teaspoons baking powder
2 eggs
⅓ cup milk
vegetable oil, for frying
salt and black pepper

Serves **4**
Prep time **10 minutes,**
plus cooling
Cooking time **25-30 minutes**

Molasses
& MUSTARD BEANS

1   Put all the ingredients into a large saucepan over low heat and bring slowly to a boil, stirring occasionally. Cover with a lid and simmer gently for 1 hour, stirring occasionally. Remove the lid and cook for another 30 minutes.

2   Toward the end of the cooking time, toast the bread in a ridged grill pan, or on a grill rack over a barbecue grill or campfire, for 2 minutes on each side until lightly charred. Rub each bread slice with a peeled garlic clove and drizzle with olive oil.

3   Serve the beans with the garlic-rubbed bread.

1 carrot, diced
1 celery stick, chopped
1 onion, chopped
2 garlic cloves, crushed
2 (15 oz) cans soybeans, drained
1 (24-28 oz) can or jar tomato
   puree tomato sauce
3 oz smoked bacon slices, diced
2 tablespoons molasses
2 teaspoons Dijon mustard
salt and black pepper

To serve
6 thick slices of sourdough
   bread
1-2 garlic cloves, peeled
olive oil, for drizzling

Serves **6**
Prep time **10 minutes**
Cooking time **1 hour 35 minutes**

CULINARY
CAMPING TIPS

Everyone expects to rough it a little when they're spending their vacation in a tent, but that doesn't mean surviving on charred toast and tepid beans for the duration. There are plenty of ways to make mealtimes occasions to look forward to, and you don't need to sacrifice too much trunk space to do it.

SPICE UP YOUR PANTRY

You won't use much in the way of herbs and spices, but a little goes a long way and you'll be surprised by the selection you can take with you if you pack carefully. You can decant dried herbs and spices—as well as condiments such as ketchup, soy sauce, and chili sauce—into small plastic bottles and containers, taking just the amount you'll need for your trip. These can be used to add instant flavor to everyday meals, such as noodles, rice dishes, omelets, baked potatoes, and stews.

CEREAL

As with condiments, there's no point filling up your food containers with big boxes of cereal—measure out the amounts you'll need and put them in smaller containers or sealable plastic bags to save on space. Alternatively, buy individual cereal servings; these also cut down on washing up, because savvy campers can add milk directly to the plastic packaging and use it as a bowl.

MORNING CUPPA

Take as many tea bags as you need (plus a few extra if tea is a staple on camping trips). If you're a coffee drinker, buy single-serving packages of instant coffee instead of taking a jar. Do the same with sugar—this will stop it from getting damp or attracting ants.

SAY CHEESE

Cheese is a camping essential. A key ingredient in everything from grilled sandwiches to omelets and a finishing flourish for pasta dishes, this should be in everyone's pantry. Hard cheeses will stay fresh if kept out of the refrigerator for a few days as long as the temperature doesn't skyrocket. To save time, grate the cheese before you leave home and keep it in an airtight container so it's ready to use when you're cooking.

INSTANT MEALTIME

Pasta and rice can take ages to cook, especially if you're relying on a campfire to get up to speed. Packages of fresh, ready-to-eat rice, pasta, and noodles are a camping cook's lifesaver that can help you create a whole range of substantial meals in a matter of minutes—and all in one saucepan.

BOSTON
Baked Beans

1 tablespoon vegetable oil
1 small red onion, finely chopped
2 celery sticks, finely chopped
1 garlic clove, crushed
¾ cup canned diced tomatoes
⅔ cup vegetable stock or broth
1 tablespoon dark soy sauce
1 tablespoon packed dark
  brown sugar
2 teaspoons Dijon mustard
2 cups drained and rinsed, canned
  navy or pinto beans
2 tablespoons chopped parsley

Serves **2**
Prep time **10 minutes**
Cooking time **30-40 minutes**

REAL HOMEMADE BAKED BEANS ARE A REVELATION.
SERVE ON TOAST OR WITH SAUSAGES.

1 Heat the oil in a saucepan, add the onion, and sauté over medium heat for about 5 minutes, until softened. Add the celery and garlic and sauté for another 1-2 minutes.

2 Add the tomatoes, stock or broth, and soy sauce. Bring to a boil, then cook at a fast simmer for about 15 minutes, or until the sauce begins to thicken.

3 Add the sugar, mustard, and beans. Continue to cook for 5 minutes, or until the beans are heated through. Stir in the chopped parsley and serve.

CAMPING TIP
Finding the right place to pitch is really important. The best spot will have morning shade and evening sunshine. The golden rule is to always choose the most level ground available but never camp on the flat next to a river.

RUSTIC PARMESAN & OLIVE BREAD

1 Put the flour, salt, pepper, yeast, oil, and cheese into a bowl and add 1 cup plus 2 tablespoons lukewarm water. Mix with a blunt knife to make a smooth dough, adding a dash more water if the dough is dry. Turn out onto a lightly floured board and knead for about 10 minutes, until the dough is smooth and elastic. Work in the olives toward the end of the kneading process. (If you've no surface to work on, work the dough in the bowl as best as you can.) Return the dough to the bowl, cover with a clean dish towel or plastic wrap, and let rest in a warm place (near the fire if already lit) until the dough has doubled in size.

2 Cut a large square of parchment paper and place over a large piece of heavy-duty aluminum foil. Punch the dough to deflate it and divide coarsely into 16 pieces. Shape each piece into a ball and space slightly apart on the paper. Position the balls in rows so you end up with a rectangular shape. Place on a baking pan. Bring the foil up around the dough and seal, then let rest again until the dough has doubled in size.

3 Slide the foil package onto a grill rack over a barbecue grill or campfire and cook the bread for about 1 hour, or until it sounds hollow when tapped on the bottom, moving the package frequently on the rack so the bread cooks evenly.

4 Carefully remove the breads from the foil package. To brown the tops, toast them on a toasting fork over the fire before serving.

3⅓ cups white bread flour, plus extra for dusting
1 teaspoon salt
½ teaspoon black pepper
2 teaspoons active dry yeast
3 tablespoons olive oil
¾ cup grated Parmesan cheese
¾ cup coarsely chopped, pitted black ripe olives

Serves **8**
Prep time **30 minutes, plus rising**
Cooking time **about 1 hour**

Summer berry GRANOLA

1 Divide the granola among bowls and pour the milk over it, then add the berries.

2 Serve with Greek yogurt and a drizzle of maple syrup.

1 quantity of Granola (see page 11)
milk, as required
1 cup mixed summer berries

To serve
Greek yogurt
maple syrup

Serves **4**
Prep time **5 minutes**

QUINOA & GOLDEN RAISIN Porridge

1 orange
1¾ cups quinoa flakes
2 cups milk
½ cup golden raisins
2 bananas
ground cinnamon (optional)
honey, to serve

Serves **4**
Prep time **10 minutes**
Cooking time **10-15 minutes**

1 Grate the zest of the orange, then peel the orange and segment the flesh. Set aside.

2 Put the quinoa flakes into a saucepan, pour in the milk and 1 cup of water, and add the golden raisins. Bring to a boil over medium heat, stirring, then simmer over low heat for 4-5 minutes, stirring frequently, until the quinoa is soft and the porridge thick and creamy.

3 Spoon the porridge into bowls immediately, because it will thicken with standing. Slice the bananas, then divide among the bowls with the orange segments. Sprinkle with the orange zest and a little ground cinnamon, if using. Serve with a drizzle of honey.

Banana & Cinnamon OATMEAL

1½ cups rolled oats
1¼ cups milk
2 bananas
¼ cup firmly packed
   light brown sugar
¼ teaspoon ground cinnamon

Serves **4**
Prep time **5 minutes**
Cooking time **10-15 minutes**

1 Put the oats into a saucepan, pour in the milk, and add 2½ cups boiling water. Bring to a boil over medium heat, stirring, then simmer over low heat for 5-6 minutes, stirring frequently, until the oats are soft and the oatmeal is thick and creamy.

2 Spoon the oatmeal into bowls, then slice the bananas and divide among the bowls. Mix together the sugar and cinnamon and sprinkle it over the top.

CORNED
BEEF HASH

6 red-skinned or white round
potatoes (about 1½ lb), peeled
and diced
3 tablespoons vegetable oil,
plus a little extra
1 large onion, chopped
2 garlic cloves, chopped
1 (12 oz) can corned beef,
chopped or crumbled
4 eggs
ketchup or barbecue sauce,
to serve (optional)

Serves **4**
Prep time **10 minutes**
Cooking time **30 minutes**

1 Cook the potatoes in a large saucepan of boiling water for about 10 minutes, until just tender. Drain well.

2 Meanwhile, heat 2 tablespoons of the oil in a skillet, add the onion and garlic, and sauté over medium-low heat for 7-8 minutes, until softened.

3 Add the remaining oil to the pan with the corned beef and drained potatoes and mix well. Continue to cook for about 15 minutes, turning occasionally—but not too often—until crispy and golden. Transfer to a large dish, cover with aluminum foil, and keep warm while you fry the eggs in the pan with a little extra oil.

4 Spoon the hash onto plates and top with the fried eggs. Serve immediately with sauce, if desired.

SAUSAGE & BACON BURGERS

THESE JUMBO BURGERS SHOULD KEEP HUNGRY CAMPERS HAPPY. IF YOU ARE FEELING EXTRA HUNGRY, ADD A FRIED EGG, TOO.

1 Put the sausagemeat into a mixing bowl and add the bacon, scallions, and apple. Sprinkle in the dry mustard and season well with salt and cayenne pepper. Stir with a spoon until well combined.

2 Divide the mixture into 4 and shape into patties, using floured hands. Cover with plastic wrap or put into a sealable plastic bag and chill in a cooler until required.

3 Brush the patties lightly with the oil and cook on a grill rack over a hot barbecue grill or campfire for 15-20 minutes, turning once or twice, until browned and cooked through. To double check, make a slit through the center of one of the burgers—there should be no hint of pink in the middle.

4 Halve the rolls and toast, cut side down, on the rack. Arrange the tomatoes over the bottom halves, add the burgers and a spoonful of ketchup, then top with the lids and serve.

1 tablespoon vegetable oil
4 ciabatta rolls or hamburger buns
3 tomatoes, sliced
ketchup

Burger mix
1 lb good-quality link sausages, skins removed
4 oz bacon slices, diced
4 scallions, finely chopped
1 apple, cored and coarsely grated (but not peeled)
1 teaspoon dry mustard
flour, for dusting
salt and cayenne pepper

Serves **4**
Prep time **15 minutes, plus chilling**
Cooking time **15-20 minutes**

Poached eggs,

BACON, & ENGLISH MUFFINS

WHEN CAMPING, POACHING THE EGGS SEPARATELY
WILL MEAN EACH SERVING IS AS HOT AS POSSIBLE.

8 thick bacon slices
2 tablespoons chopped basil
2 tablespoons olive oil
4 tomatoes, thickly sliced
4 English muffins
4 extra-large eggs
1 tablespoon vinegar
butter, for spreading
salt and black pepper

Serves **4**
Prep time **5 minutes**
Cooking time **20 minutes**

1 Heat a skillet over medium heat, then add the bacon slices and dry-fry for 6-8 minutes, turning once, until cooked through. Push to the side of the pan.

2 Mix together the basil and oil in a bowl. Add the tomato slices to the skillet and drizzle with the basil oil. Season well with salt and black pepper, then cook for 3-4 minutes, until starting to soften.

3 Meanwhile, halve the English muffins and toast in a ridged grill pan or on a grill rack over a barbecue grill or campfire. Wrap in a clean dish towel and keep warm.

4 Bring a large saucepan of water to a boil. Break 1 of the eggs into a cup, making sure not to break the yolk. Add the vinegar to the boiling water, then stir the water rapidly in a circular motion to make a whirlpool. Carefully slide the egg into the center of the pan while the water is still swirling, holding the cup as close to the water as you can. Cook for about 3 minutes, then lift out with a slotted spoon.

5 Butter 2 halves of an English muffin. Top the bottom half with one-quarter of the tomato slices, 2 slices of bacon, and the poached egg, then top with the lid and serve.

6 Cook and serve the other 3 eggs in the same way, swirling the boiling water into a whirlpool each time before sliding in the egg.

BBQ & CAMPFIRE

40 CLASSIC HAMBURGERS

41 FAST-SEARED STEAKS WITH
    GREEN BEANS

42 SPICY THAI HAMBURGERS

44 SUGAR & SPICE GLAZED BEEF

45 GREEN PEPPERCORN STEAKS

46 BUTTERFLIED LEG OF LAMB WITH
    FAVA BEAN & DILL YOGURT

47 AROMATIC BARBECUED LAMB

47 TAVERNA-STYLE LAMB WITH
    FETA SALAD

48 MINTED LAMB KEBABS

49 BARBECUED PORK SPARERIBS

50 PORK CUTLETS WITH
    LEMON & CAPERS

51 HAM STEAKS WITH
    CARAMELIZED ONIONS

52 CHORIZO & QUAIL EGG PIZZAS

53 SEARED PORK CHOPS WITH
    SPICY CORN

54 SPIT-ROASTED PORK WITH
    APPLE BUTTER

55 CHICKEN SATAY SKEWERS

56 LEMON & PARSLEY
    CHICKEN SKEWERS

57 TANDOORI CHICKEN SKEWERS
    WITH CUCUMBER & CUMIN SALAD

58 BLACKENED CHICKEN SKEWERS

59 CHICKEN BURGERS WITH
    TOMATO SALSA

60 CHICKEN & MOZZARELLA SKEWERS

62 HERB-MARINATED
    BUTTERFLIED CHICKEN

63 SPIT-ROASTED CHICKEN
    WITH SAFFRON MAYONNAISE

64 CHICKEN FAJITAS

66 THAI BARBECUED CHICKEN

67 SHRIMP & BACON SKEWERS

68 SCALLOP & CHORIZO SKEWERS

69 QUICK TUNA STEAKS WITH
    GREEN SALSA

70 BLACKENED TUNA WITH
    MANGO SALSA

72 SWORDFISH STEAKS WITH BASIL
    & PINE NUT OIL

73 OLIVE & CITRUS SALMON

74 STUFFED SALMON FILLETS
    WITH PANCETTA & TOMATOES

75 MACKEREL WITH CITRUS
    FENNEL SALAD

TOMATO, PESTO, & OLIVE PIZZAS

SEASONED
JUMBO SHRIMP

PORK SPARERIBS

CLASSIC HAMBURGERS

olive oil, for brushing
4 hamburger buns
2 tablespoons mustard
shredded lettuce
2 tomatoes, sliced
2 dill pickles, sliced

Burger mix
1 lb ground chuck beef
8 oz ground pork
1 onion, finely chopped
1 teaspoon Worcestershire
  sauce
2 tablespoons capers, drained
salt and black pepper

Serves **4**
Prep time **10 minutes,**
plus chilling
Cooking time **10-12 minutes**

1 Put the ground beef, ground pork, onion, Worcestershire sauce, capers, salt, and black pepper in a bowl. Mix together well, using your hands. Divide the mixture into 4 and shape into even patties. Cover with plastic wrap or put in a sealable plastic bag and chill in a cooler for 30 minutes.

2 Brush the patties lightly with oil and cook on a grill rack over a hot barbecue grill or campfire for 5-6 minutes on each side, or until lightly charred and cooked through.

3 Meanwhile, halve the buns and toast on both sides on the rack. Spread the bottom halves with a little mustard, then fill with the shredded lettuce, burgers, tomato slices, and dill pickles. Top with the lids and serve.

FAST-SEARED STEAKS
WITH **GREEN BEANS**

1 Cook the green beans in a saucepan of lightly salted boiling water for 3-4 minutes, or until tender but firm.

2 Meanwhile, to make the tomato dressing, mix together all the ingredients in a small bowl.

3 Drain the beans and return to the pan. Toss the tomato dressing through the beans, season well with salt and black pepper, cover with a lid, and keep warm.

4 Rub the oil over the steaks, then cook on a rack over a hot barbecue grill or campfire for 1 minute on each side, or until cooked to your preference. Transfer to a plate, cover with aluminum foil, and let rest for 1-2 minutes.

5 Divide the arugula among the plates. Spoon the beans and dressing over the greens, then top with the steaks. Serve immediately with crusty bread.

4 cups trimmed green beans
   (about 12 oz)
1 teaspoon olive oil
4 thin steaks, such as hanger
   steaks or skirt steaks
1 (5 oz) package arugula
salt and black pepper
crusty bread, to serve

Tomato dressing
2 tomatoes, diced
1 teaspoon olive oil
1 banana shallot, finely chopped
1 tablespoon whole-grain
   mustard
1 tablespoon red wine vinegar

Serves **4**
Prep time **10 minutes**
Cooking time **5 minutes**

SPICY *Thai* HAMBURGERS

olive oil, for brushing
1 baguette or other long
   thin roll, cut into 4 and
   split lengthwise
shredded lettuce
sweet chili sauce

Burger mix
1 lb ground chuck beef
1 tablespoon Thai red curry
   paste
½ cup fresh white bread
   crumbs
2 tablespoons chopped fresh
   cilantro
1 egg, lightly beaten
1 tablespoon light soy sauce
black pepper

Serves **4**
Prep time **10 minutes**
Cooking time **10 minutes**

1 Put the ground beef into a bowl and stir in the red curry paste, bread crumbs, cilantro, egg, soy sauce, and black pepper. Mix together well using your hands. Divide the mixture into 8 and shape into mini patties.

2 Brush the patties lightly with oil and cook on a grill rack over a hot barbecue grill or campfire for 4–5 minutes on each side, or until charred and cooked through.

3 Serve the burgers in the split bread with shredded lettuce and sweet chili sauce.

SUGAR & SPICE GLAZED BEEF

8 juniper berries
3 tablespoons molasses
2 tablespoons packed
   light brown sugar
2 tablespoons whiskey
2 tablespoons Worcestershire
   sauce
1 tablespoon whole-grain
   mustard
½ teaspoon black pepper
1¼ lb tenderloin steak
salt

Serves **4-5**
Prep time **10 minutes,**
plus marinating
Cooking time **about 30 mins**

1 Crush the juniper berries using a mortar and pestle. Mix in a bowl with the molasses, sugar, whiskey, Worcestershire sauce, mustard, and black pepper. Put the steak into a nonmetallic dish and pour the marinade all over the surface. Cover loosely with plastic wrap and marinate in your cooler for about 1 hour.

2 Lift the meat from the dish, letting the excess marinade drip back into the dish, and season with a little salt. Transfer to a grill rack over a barbecue grill or campfire and cook for about 30 minutes, turning the meat frequently so it cooks fairly evenly. Use a meat thermometer to test whether the beef is cooked to your preference. For rare the temperature should register about 120°F. For well done, the meal should register 158-165°F and will take longer to cook.

3 Pour the marinade juices into a small saucepan and heat through on the rack beside the meat. Transfer the meat to a board and carve into thick slices. Serve drizzled with the juices.

CAMPING TIP

If the weather forecast is for rain, the golden rule of pitching on flat ground can be wavered and you should pitch your tent on a slight incline or on the highest part of the site so it doesn't flood—there's nothing worse than waking up in a soggy sleeping bag.

Green PEPPERCORN STEAKS

1 Heat a ridged grill pan on a grill rack over a hot barbecue grill or campfire until hot.

2 Meanwhile, cook the steaks on the grill rack for 2-3 minutes on each side, or until cooked to your preference. Transfer to a plate, cover with aluminum foil, and let rest while you make the sauce.

3 Put the peppercorns, soy sauce, balsamic vinegar, and cherry tomatoes into the ridged grill pan. Let the liquids sizzle for a few minutes or until the tomatoes are soft. Spoon the sauce over the steaks and serve.

4 lean tenderloin steaks, about 3 oz each
1 tablespoon green peppercorns in liquid, drained
2 tablespoons light soy sauce
1 teaspoon balsamic vinegar
8 cherry tomatoes, halved

Serves 4
Prep time **5 minutes**
Cooking time **about 10 minutes**

BUTTERFLIED
LEG OF LAMB
with Fava Bean & Dill Yogurt

5 garlic cloves, crushed
4 handfuls of mint leaves, chopped
4 handfuls of parsley, chopped
3 tablespoons green peppercorns in liquid, drained and crushed
2 tablespoons olive oil
1 butterflied leg of lamb (about 3½ lb)

Fava bean and dill yogurt
²/₃ cup fresh baby fava beans
1 cup Greek yogurt
¼ cup chopped dill
salt

Serves **6**
Prep time **15 minutes**, **plus marinating**
Cooking time **30-40 minutes**

1 Mix together the garlic, mint, parsley, peppercorns, and oil. Open out the lamb and spread the herb mixture all over the surface of the lamb. Place in a nonmetallic dish and cover loosely with plastic wrap. Let marinate for several hours or overnight in the cooler, allowing the meat to sit at room temperature for a couple of hours before cooking.

2 To make the yogurt, cook the beans in a saucepan of boiling water for 3-5 minutes, until tender. Drain and let cool. Pop the beans out of their skins and mix with the yogurt, dill, and a little salt. Transfer to a serving dish.

3 Transfer the lamb to a grill rack over a hot barbecue grill or campfire and cook for 15-20 minutes on each side, or until thoroughly browned on the outside but still pink in the middle.

4 Place on a serving board or plate, cover with aluminum foil, and let rest for 15 minutes before slicing. Serve with the yogurt.

COOKING TIP
Cook the meat where the heat is least intense and for longer if you prefer lamb cooked through.

AROMATIC **BARBECUED** LAMB

1 Place the lamb chops in a shallow, nonmetallic dish. Mix the ginger with the garlic, chile, sugar, soy sauce, and sherry and pour it over the lamb.

2 Turn the meat in the mixture, cover with plastic wrap, and chill in a cooler for at least 2 hours or overnight.

3 Transfer the chops to a grill rack over a hot barbecue grill or campfire and cook for 3–8 minutes on each side, depending on whether you like the meat rare or well done. Use any excess marinade to baste the meat while it is cooking.

4 Serve with baked new potatoes.

4 lamb chops
3/4 inch piece of fresh ginger root, peeled and grated
2 garlic cloves, crushed
1 red chile, seeded and thinly sliced
2 teaspoons packed dark brown sugar
3 tablespoons soy sauce
2 tablespoons dry sherry
Fire-Baked New Potatoes (see page 203), to serve

Serves **4**
Prep time **10 minutes**
Cooking time **10-15 minutes**

Taverna-Style LAMB WITH FETA SALAD

2 tablespoons chopped oregano
1 tablespoon chopped rosemary
grated zest of 1 lemon
2 tablespoons olive oil
salt and black pepper
1 lb leg or shoulder of lamb, diced
crusty bread, to serve (optional)

Feta salad
7 oz feta cheese, sliced
1 tablespoon chopped oregano
2 tablespoons chopped parsley
grated zest and juice of 1 lemon
1/2 small red onion, finely sliced
3 tablespoons olive oil

Serves **4**
Prep time **15 minutes**
Cooking time **about 8 minutes**

1 Mix together the herbs, lemon zest, oil, and salt and black pepper in a nonmetallic dish, add the lamb, and mix to coat thoroughly. Thread the meat onto 4 metal skewers.

2 Arrange the sliced feta on a large serving dish and sprinkle with the herbs, lemon zest, and sliced onion. Drizzle with the lemon juice and oil and season with salt and black pepper.

3 Cook the lamb skewers on a grill rack over a hot barbecue grill or campfire for 6–8 minutes, turning frequently, until charred on the outside and almost cooked through. Transfer to a plate, cover with aluminum foil, and let rest for 1–2 minutes.

4 Serve the lamb, with any pan juices poured over, with the salad and plenty of crusty bread, if desired.

MINTED LAMB KEBABS

1 lb ground lamb
1 small onion, finely chopped
1 garlic clove, crushed
1 tablespoon chopped rosemary
6 anchovies in oil, drained and
  chopped
olive oil, for brushing
salt and black pepper

Tomato and olive salad
6 tomatoes, cut into wedges
1 red onion, sliced
1 cup pitted black ripe olives
a few torn basil leaves
2 tablespoons olive oil
a squeeze of lemon juice

1 Put the lamb, chopped onion, garlic, rosemary, anchovies, and some salt and black pepper into a bowl and mix together using your hands. Divide the mixture into 12 and shape into even cylinderical shapes. Cover with plastic wrap and chill in the cooler for 30 minutes.

2 Thread the lamb onto metal skewers, brush lightly with oil, and cook on a grill rack over a hot barbecue grill or campfire for 3-4 minutes on each side, or until cooked through.

3 Meanwhile, to make the salad, put the tomatoes, onion, olives, and basil into a bowl, season with salt and black pepper, and mix together. Drizzle with oil and squeeze with a little lemon juice. Serve the kebabs with the salad.

Serves **4**
Prep time **15 minutes,**
plus chilling
Cooking time **about 7 minutes**

BARBECUED PORK
Spareribs

½ cup ketchup
2 tablespoons honey
1 tablespoon dark soy sauce
1 tablespoon olive oil
1 tablespoon malt vinegar
2 teaspoons Dijon mustard
4 lb pork spareribs
salt and black pepper

1 Mix together all the ingredients except the pork in a bowl, then coat the ribs generously all over with the marinade.

2 Transfer to a grill rack over a barbecue grill or campfire and cook for 20-30 minutes, basting occasionally with the marinade and turning frequently, until charred and tender.

Serves **4**
Prep time **5 minutes**
Cooking time **20-30 minutes**

PORK CUTLETS
WITH LEMON & CAPERS

1 tablespoon chopped flat leaf parsley

3 tablespoons chopped mint

¼–⅓ cup lemon juice

1 tablespoon capers, drained and chopped

⅓ cup olive oil, plus extra for brushing

4 pork cutlets (about 4 oz each), trimmed

1 Mix together the herbs, lemon juice, capers, and oil in a bowl.

2 Brush the pork with oil and cook on a grill rack over a hot barbecue grill or campfire for 2–3 minutes on each side, or until cooked through.

3 Drizzle the lemon and caper dressing over the pork and serve.

Serves **4**
Prep time **10 minutes**
Cooking time **about 5 minutes**

CAMPING TIP
Bring collapsible storage containers for flexible storage while you're on site. They can be used for shoes and boots, firewood, or keeping the tent clutter free. And they barely take up any space once they're folded away.

Ham Steaks WITH CARAMELIZED ONIONS

1 Melt the butter in a skillet, add the onions and thyme, and cook over low heat, stirring occasionally, for about 15 minutes, until softened and beginning to caramelize. Stir in the marmalade, mustard, and stock or broth and bring to a boil, then simmer gently for 2–3 minutes, until beginning to thicken.

2 Meanwhile, brush the ham steaks with the oil and cook on a grill rack over a barbecue grill or campfire for about 15 minutes, turning once, until cooked through.

3 Add the steaks to the sauce and simmer for another 3 minutes, until the sauce is thick and sticky and the steaks are piping hot. Serve with instant mashed potatoes, if desired.

a pat of butter
2 onions, sliced
2 teaspoons thyme leaves
¼ cup marmalade
1 tablespoon whole-grain mustard
1¼ cups hot chicken stock or broth
4 lean cured ham steaks (about 4 oz each)
1 tablespoon olive oil
instant mashed potatoes, to serve (optional)

Serves **4**
Prep time **5 minutes**
Cooking time **25 minutes**

CHORIZO
& Quail Egg PIZZAS

1 cup plus 2 tablespoons
  white bread flour, plus extra
  for dusting
½ teaspoon active dry yeast
½ teaspoon salt
1 tablespoon olive oil

Topping
2 tablespoons olive oil, plus
  extra for drizzling
1 small garlic clove, crushed
3 oz thinly sliced chorizo
  sausage
1 red chile, seeded and halved
1¼ cups grated Manchego
  cheese
2 tablespoons pine nuts
6 quail eggs
salt and black pepper
arugula, to serve

Serves 2
Prep time **25 minutes,
plus rising**
Cooking time **about
30 minutes**

1 To make the pizza crust, mix the flour, yeast, salt, and olive oil in a bowl and add ⅓ cup lukewarm water. Mix with a blunt knife to make a soft dough, adding a dash more water if the dough is dry. Turn out onto a floured board and knead for about 10 minutes, until the dough is smooth and elastic. (If you've no surface to work on, knead the dough in the bowl as best as you can.) Return the dough to the bowl, cover with a clean dish towel or plastic wrap, and let rest in a warm place (near the fire if already lit) until the dough has doubled in size.

2 Heat a sturdy baking sheet on a rack over a barbecue grill or campfire while assembling the pizza. Mix together the olive oil and garlic in a bowl.

3 Turn the dough out onto a floured surface and cut in half. Thinly roll out each piece to an oval shape measuring about 8½ x 5½ inches or to a size that allows you to fit them side by side on the baking sheet. Transfer to the baking sheet and brush with the garlic oil. Sprinkle with the chorizo and add a chile half to each. Sprinkle with the cheese and pine nuts and make 3 small indentations in each topping, then break the eggs into the wells and season with salt and black pepper.

4 Make a dome of aluminum foil and position over the pizzas, tucking the ends under the bottoms to secure. Cook for about 30 minutes, or until the crusts are cooked and the eggs are softly set. Rotate the pizzas on the rack several times during cooking. Serve sprinkled with arugula and an extra drizzle of oil.

Seared PORK CHOPS
WITH SPICY CORN

1 Brush the chops with half the oil and cook on a grill rack over a barbecue grill or campfire for 5-10 minutes on each side (depending on thickness), or until golden and cooked through. Keep warm and let rest for 5 minutes.

2 Meanwhile, to make the spicy corn, heat the remaining oil in a skillet, add the corn, and cook for 2 minutes, until starting to brown, then stir in the scallions and chile and cook for another 1 minute. Add the créme fraîche or sour cream and lime zest and season with salt and black pepper. Sprinkle with the cilantro and serve with the pork chops.

2 tablespoons olive oil
4 pork chops
1½ cups canned corn kernels
2 scallions, thinly sliced
1 red chile, chopped
⅓ cup créme fraîche
  or sour cream
finely grated zest of 1 lime
handful of cilantro leaves,
  chopped
salt and black pepper

Serves **4**
Prep time **10 minutes**
Cooking time **10-20 minutes**

Spit-Roasted Pork
WITH APPLE BUTTER

IF YOU DON'T HAVE SPIT-ROASTING EQUIPMENT, ROAST THE PORK ON A GRILL RACK OVER THE FIRE, TURNING IT FREQUENTLY UNTIL COOKED THROUGH. WRAP THE MEAT IN ALUMINUM FOIL TO FINISH COOKING IF IT STARTS TO BURN.

1 Mix together the fennel seeds, caraway seeds, garlic, lemon zest, black pepper, and a little salt in a bowl. Make plenty of cuts over the surface of the meat with the tip of a sharp knife, then push some of the spice mixture into the cuts and spread the remainder all over the surface. Roll up and tie the pork at 1¼ inch intervals with kitchen string.

2 Skewer the pork onto a spit-roasting rod and set up over a campfire or barbecue grill. Roast for 3–4 hours, or until the pork is cooked through. Test the pork is cooked by pushing a meat thermometer into the thickest area of the meat. It should read about 165°F.

3 To make the butter, chop the apples into pieces and put in a saucepan with a dash of water. Cover with a lid and cook on the rack to one side of the pork until the apples are tender. You'll need to frequently add more water to stop the apples from burning on the bottom of the pan before they're soft. Once soft and mushy, remove from the heat, stir in the cloves, sugar, and lemon juice, and let cool. Add the butter to the cooled apple mixture and beat well to mix.

4 Transfer the pork to a plate or board. Cover with aluminum foil and let rest in a warm place near the barbecue or fire for 15 minutes before removing the string. Carve into thick slices and serve in rolls, baguettes, or soft wraps with the apple butter.

2 teaspoons fennel seeds, lightly crushed
2 teaspoons caraway seeds, lightly crushed
4 garlic cloves, crushed
finely grated zest of 2 lemons
1 teaspoon black pepper
4 lb shoulder of pork, skin and excess fat removed
salt
rolls, baguettes, or soft wraps, to serve

Apple butter
3 cooking apples, such as Granny Smith (about 1 lb), peeled, quartered, and cored
pinch of ground cloves
1 teaspoon sugar
squeeze of lemon juice
4 tablespoons salted butter, softened

Serves 6
Prep time **25 minutes**
Cooking time **3–4 hours**

CHICKEN SATAY
SKEWERS

1 Soak 8 wooden skewers in cold water for 30 minutes. Mix together the soy sauce, oil, and 5-spice powder in a bowl. Add the chicken strips and toss together to coat in the marinade. Cover with plastic wrap and let marinate in the cooler for 1 hour, stirring occasionally.

2 Thread the chicken, zigzag fashion, onto the soaked skewers. Transfer to a grill rack over a hot barbecue grill or campfire and cook for about 10 minutes, turning once, until golden and cooked through.

3 Meanwhile, put the sauce ingredients in a small saucepan with $1/2$ cup of water and heat, stirring, until warm and well mixed. Transfer to a small serving bowl.

4 Serve the hot chicken skewers with the satay sauce and cucumber strips.

$1/3$ cup dark soy sauce
2 tablespoons vegetable oil
1 teaspoon Chinese 5-spice
  powder
2–3 boneless, skinless chicken
  breasts (about 12 oz), cut into
  long, thin strips
cucumber, cut into strips,
  to serve

Satay sauce
$1/4$ cup peanut butter
1 tablespoon dark soy sauce
$1/2$ teaspoon ground coriander
$1/2$ teaspoon ground cumin
pinch of paprika or chili powder

Serves **4**
Prep time **20 minutes,**
plus marinating
Cooking time **10 minutes**

Lemon & Parsley
CHICKEN SKEWERS

2 boneless, skinless chicken
  breasts (about 10 oz),
  cut into chunks
finely grated zest and juice of
  1 lemon
2 tablespoons olive oil
3 tablespoons finely
  chopped parsley
salt and black pepper

To serve
arugula and tomato salad
warm pita breads
1 cup cucumber yogurt dip

Serves **2**
Prep time **15 minutes**
Cooking time **10-15 minutes**

1 Put the chicken into a bowl with the lemon zest and juice and
  the oil and toss well to coat. Stir in the parsley and season
well with salt and black pepper.

2 Thread the chicken onto 4 small metal skewers. Transfer
  to a grill rack over a hot barbecue grill or campfire
and cook for 10-15 minutes, turning once, until golden and
cooked through.

3 Remove from the skewers and serve in warm pita breads
  with a simple arugula and tomato salad and spoonfuls of
a cucumber yogurt dip.

TANDOORI CHICKEN SKEWERS
with cucumber & cumin salad

¾ cup Greek yogurt, plus extra
    to serve
2 tablespoons tandoori paste
3-4 boneless, skinless chicken
    breasts (about 1 lb), cut into
    thin strips
2 lemons, cut into wedges
mini naans or other flat breads,
    to serve (optional)

Cucumber salad
2 teaspoons cumin seeds
1 small cucumber
1 red onion, halved and
    finely sliced
3 tablespoons cilantro leaves
salt and black pepper

Serves **4**
Prep time **15 minutes,
plus marinating**
Cooking time **12 minutes**

1 Mix together the yogurt and tandoori paste in a bowl, add the chicken, and toss until the chicken is well coated. Cover with plastic wrap and let marinate for 10 minutes.

2 Heat a skillet over medium heat, add the cumin seeds, and dry-roast for 1-2 minutes, stirring frequently. Remove from the heat when the seeds become fragrant and begin to smoke.

3 Thread the chicken strips onto 8 small metal skewers. Transfer to a grill rack over a hot barbecue grill or campfire and cook for about 10 minutes, turning once, until cooked through.

4 Meanwhile, slice the cucumber into ribbons, using a sharp vegetable peeler, and arrange on plates. Sprinkle the onion and cilantro over the cucumber, sprinkle with the toasted cumin seeds, and season lightly with salt and black pepper. Place the chicken on top and serve with lemon wedges, extra yogurt, and warm naans, if desired.

BLACKENED
CHICKEN
SKEWERS

2 boneless, skinless chicken breasts (about 10 oz), cut into chunks
1 tablespoon Cajun seasoning mix
2 tablespoons lemon juice
1 teaspoon olive oil

To serve
Garlic Bread (see page 206)
green salad

Serves **4**
Prep time **5 minutes, plus marinating**
Cooking time **10-15 minutes**

1 Soak 8 wooden skewers in cold water for 30 minutes. Put the chicken in a bowl, add the seasoning mix, lemon juice, and olive oil, and toss together well. Cover with plastic wrap and let marinate for 15 minutes.

2 Thread the chicken onto the soaked skewers. Transfer to a grill rack over a hot barbecue grill or campfire and cook for 10-15 minutes, turning once, until cooked through.

3 Serve with garlic bread and a green salad.

CAMPING TIP

Washing soda is good for cleaning your barbecue. Simply mix a couple of tablespoons of powder into some hot water and scrub off the remains of last night's burger feast. If you have a large container, you can soak the grill rack in the liquid overnight to soften the grease and the results will be even better.

CHICKEN BURGERS
WITH TOMATO SALSA

1 Mix together all the burger ingredients except the oil in a bowl. Divide the mixture into 4 and shape into even flattened patties. Cover with plastic wrap and chill in a cooler for 30 minutes.

2 Meanwhile, combine all the tomato salsa ingredients together in a bowl.

3 Brush the patties lightly with the oil and cook on a grill rack over a hot barbecue grill or campfire for 3-4 minutes on each side, or until cooked through. Serve immediately with the salsa.

1 garlic clove, crushed
3 scallions, finely sliced
1 tablespoon pesto
2 tablespoons chopped fresh mixed herbs, such as parsley, tarragon, and thyme
12 oz ground chicken
2 sun-dried tomatoes, finely chopped
1 teaspoon olive oil

Tomato salsa
15 cherry tomatoes, quartered
1 red chile, cored, seeded, and finely chopped
1 tablespoon chopped fresh cilantro
grated zest and juice of 1 lime

Serves **4**
Prep time **15 minutes, plus chilling**
Cooking time **6-8 minutes**

CHICKEN & MOZZARELLA SKEWERS

8 small boneless, skinless
chicken thighs
2 bocconcini balls (baby
mozzarellas), quartered
8 large basil leaves
8 large slices of prosciutto
2 small lemons, halved
salt and black pepper

Serves 4
Prep time **15 minutes**
Cooking time **20 minutes**

1 Lay the chicken thighs flat on a plate, boned side up, and season with a little salt and black pepper. Place one-quarter of a bocconcini and a basil leaf in the center of each, then roll up to enclose the filling. Wrap each thigh in a slice of prosciutto and thread onto 8 metal skewers, using 2 skewers for 2 packages (this makes them easier to turn).

2 Transfer the skewers to a grill rack over a hot barbecue grill or campfire and cook for about 8 minutes on each side, or until cooked through and the mozzarella starts to ooze. Transfer to a plate, cover with aluminum foil, and let rest for 5 minutes.

3 Meanwhile, cook the lemon halves, cut side down, for 5 minutes, until charred and tender. Serve the skewers drizzled with the lemon juice.

HERB-MARINATED
Butterflied Chicken

1 teaspoon cumin seeds,
   lightly crushed
2 garlic cloves, crushed
2 handfuls of parsley, chopped
2 handfuls of cilantro leaves,
   chopped
¼ teaspoon dried red
   pepper flakes
1 tablespoon vegetable oil
1 tablespoon honey
finely grated zest of 1 lemon
2 teaspoons lemon juice
1 whole chicken (about 3 lb)
salt

To serve
leafy salad
new potatoes

Serves **4**
Prep time **20 minutes,**
plus marinating
Cooking time **about**
40 minutes

1 Mix together the cumin seeds, garlic, parsley, cilantro, dried red pepper flakes, oil, honey, and lemon zest and juice in a bowl.

2 To butterfly the chicken, place the chicken on a board, breast side down. Using sturdy kitchen scissors, cut along one side of the backbone, then the other to remove the backbone completely. Turn the bird over, breast side up, and flatten out the legs so they face inward. Use the heel of your hand to push the breastbone firmly down and flatten out the chicken completely.

3 Push a wooden skewer diagonally through the bird so the skewer goes through one leg then out through the wing on the other side. Push another skewer through in the opposite direction. Spread the herb mixture over the chicken on both sides and place on a plate. Cover loosely with plastic wrap and let marinate in a cooler for several hours.

4 Season the chicken lightly with salt on both sides. Transfer to a grill rack over a barbecue grill or campfire and cook for about 20 minutes on each side, or until the juices run clear when the thickest part of the chicken is pierced with a sharp knife. If the chicken skin starts to burn before the chicken is cooked through, wrap it in aluminum foil and move to one side of the rack so it can cook more gently.

5 Transfer the chicken to a large board or plate, cover with foil, and let rest for 5 minutes, then chop the chicken into pieces and serve with salad and new potatoes.

SPIT-ROASTED CHICKEN
WITH SAFFRON MAYONNAISE

IF YOU DON'T HAVE SPIT-ROASTING EQUIPMENT, ROAST THE CHICKEN ON A GRILL RACK OVER A BARBECUE GRILL OR CAMPFIRE, TURNING IT FREQUENTLY UNTIL COOKED THROUGH. IF THE SKIN STARTS TO BURN, WRAP THE CHICKEN IN ALUMINUM FOIL TO FINISH COOKING. BUTTERFLYING THE CHICKEN FIRST (SEE PAGE 62) WILL HELP SPEED UP COOKING TIME.

1 Put the paprika, fennel seeds, celery seeds, garlic, and black pepper into a large plastic freezer bag and shake the bag to mix the ingredients together. Add the chicken to the bag. Balloon out the bag, twisting the open end to secure, and turn the chicken in the spice mixture until coated. Tie loosely and let marinate in a cooler for several hours or overnight.

2 Push the herbs into the chicken cavity. Skewer the chicken onto a spit-roasting rod and set up over a barbecue grill or campfire. Sprinkle with a little salt and roast for 1½–2 hours, or until the chicken is cooked through. The juices should run clear when the thickest part of the thigh is pierced with a sharp knife.

3 To make the mayonnaise, crumble the saffron into a mug and add 1 teaspoon boiling water. Let stand for 5 minutes. Beat the crème fraîche or yogurt and mayonnaise together in a bowl with a little salt and black pepper. Stir in the saffron and liquid.

4 Transfer the chicken to a plate or board and cover with aluminum foil. Let rest in a warm place near the barbecue or fire for 15 minutes before carving. Serve with the mayonnaise.

2 teaspoons ground paprika
1 teaspoon fennel seeds, lightly crushed
½ teaspoon celery seeds
2 garlic cloves, finely chopped
½ teaspoon black pepper
1 whole chicken (about 3 lb)
small handful of bay leaves, thyme, and parsley
salt

Saffron mayonnaise
good pinch of saffron strands
½ cup crème fraîche or Greek yogurt
½ cup mayonnaise

Serves 4
Prep time **15 minutes, plus marinating**
Cooking time 1½–**2 hours**

½ teaspoon ground coriander
½ teaspoon ground cumin
½ teaspoon ground paprika
1 garlic clove, crushed
3 tablespoons chopped
  fresh cilantro
2-3 boneless, skinless chicken
  breasts (about 12 oz, cut into
  bite-size strips)
1 tablespoon olive oil
4 soft flour tortillas
sour cream, to serve (optional)

Salsa

3 large ripe tomatoes, finely
  chopped
3 tablespoons chopped fresh
  cilantro
⅛ cucumber, finely chopped
1 tablespoon olive oil

Guacamole

1 large avocado, peeled, pitted,
  and coarsely chopped
grated zest and juice of ½ lime
2 teaspoons sweet chili sauce
  (optional)

Serves 4
Prep time **20 minutes**
Cooking time **about 5 minutes**

CHICKEN FAJITAS

1 Put all the ground spices, garlic, and chopped cilantro into a bowl. Toss the chicken in the oil, then add to the spices and toss to coat lightly in the spice mixture. Cover with plastic wrap and let marinate while you make the salsa.

2 To make the salsa, mix together the tomatoes, cilantro, and cucumber in a bowl and drizzle with the oil.

3 To make the guacamole, in a separate bowl, mash together the avocado, lime zest and juice, and sweet chili sauce, if using, until soft and a coarse texture.

4 Heat a ridged grill pan or skillet on a grill rack over a barbecue grill or campfire until hot, add the chicken, and cook for about 5 minutes, turning occasionally, until golden and cooked through.

5 Fill the tortillas with the hot chicken strips, guacamole, and salsa. Fold into quarters and serve with a little sour cream, if desired.

THAI BARBECUED
CHICKEN

1 whole chicken (about 3 lb),
   butterflied (see page 62)
2 inch piece of fresh galangal
   or ginger root, peeled and
   finely chopped
4 garlic cloves, crushed
1 large red chile, finely chopped
4 shallots, finely chopped
2 tablespoons finely chopped
   fresh cilantro
2/3 cup canned coconut milk
salt and black pepper

To serve
sweet chili sauce
lime wedges
boiled rice

Serves 4
Prep time **20 minutes,
plus marinating**
Cooking time **about
40 minutes**

1 Rub the chicken all over with salt and black pepper and place in a shallow dish. Mix together the remaining ingredients in a bowl until well blended, then pour the marinade over the chicken. Cover loosely with plastic wrap and let marinate in a cooler for several hours or overnight.

2 Transfer the chicken from the marinade to a grill rack over a hot barbecue grill or campfire and cook for about 20 minutes on each side, turning and basting frequently with the remaining marinade, until the juices run clear when the thickest part of the chicken is pierced with a sharp knife. If the chicken skin starts to burn before the chicken is cooked through, wrap it in aluminum foil and move to one side of the rack so it can cook more gently.

3 Transfer the chicken to a large board or plate, cover with foil, and let rest for 5 minutes, then chop it into small pieces. Serve with sweet chili sauce, lime wedges, and boiled rice.

COOKING TIP
If you prefer, use 4 part-boned chicken breasts. Follow the recipe instructions above, but cook the chicken for only 10–15 minutes, or until cooked through.

SHRIMP & BACON
SKEWERS

1 Soak 12 wooden skewers in cold water for 30 minutes. Cut each bacon slice into 3 pieces widthwise, then run the back of a knife along the length of each piece to stretch them out thinly.

2 Wrap each shrimp carefully with bacon and thread onto a soaked skewer with a tomato and basil leaf. Season each skewer with a little salt and black pepper.

3 Brush the skewers with a little oil and cook on grill rack over a hot barbecue grill or campfire for 2-3 minutes on each side, or until the shrimp turn pink and are cooked through. Serve hot with the lemon wedges for squeezing over the shrimp.

4 bacon slices
12 raw large shrimp, peeled and
   deveined but tails intact
12 cherry tomatoes
12 basil leaves
olive oil, for brushing
salt and black pepper
lemon wedges, to serve

Serves **4**
Prep time **10 minutes,
plus soaking**
Cooking time **4-6 minutes**

SCALLOP & CHORIZO
SKEWERS

12 scallops, white meat only
12 large sage leaves
5 oz chorizo sausage, cut into
    twelve ½ inch pieces
2 tablespoons olive oil
1 tablespoon lemon juice
1 garlic clove, crushed
salt and black pepper
lemon wedges, to serve

Serves **4**
Prep time **10 minutes, plus
soaking and marinating**
Cooking time **4-6 minutes**

1 Soak 12 small wooden skewers in cold water for 30 minutes. Wrap each scallop with a sage leaf and thread onto the soaked skewers with the pieces of chorizo, then transfer to a dish.

2 Mix together the oil, lemon juice, garlic, and salt and black pepper in a bowl, then drizzle the marinade over the skewers. Cover with plastic wrap and let marinate in a cooler for 1 hour.

3 Cook the skewers on a grill rack over a hot barbecue grill or campfire for 2-3 minutes on each side, or until the scallops are cooked though. Serve hot with lemon wedges for squeezing over the scallops.

QUICK TUNA STEAKS
with green salsa

2 tablespoons olive oil
grated zest of 1 lemon
2 teaspoons chopped parsley
½ teaspoon crushed coriander
   seeds
4 tuna steaks (about 5 oz each)
salt and black pepper
crusty bread, to serve

Salsa
2 tablespoons capers, drained
   and chopped
2 tablespoons chopped pickles
1 tablespoon finely chopped
   parsley
2 teaspoons chopped chives
2 teaspoons finely chopped
   chervil
¼ cup chopped pitted
   green olives
1 shallot, finely chopped
   (optional)
2 tablespoons lemon juice
2 tablespoons olive oil

Serves **4**
Prep time **15 minutes**
Cooking time **2–4 minutes**

1 Mix together the oil, lemon zest, parsley, coriander seeds, and plenty of black pepper in a bowl. Rub the tuna steaks with the mixture and set aside.

2 To make the salsa, mix together the ingredients in a bowl, season with salt and black pepper, and set aside.

3 Cook the tuna on a grill rack over a hot barbecue grill or campfire for 1–2 minutes on each side, or until well charred on the outside but still pink in the middle. Alternatively, cook for a little less time, or for longer, until cooked to your preference.

4 Transfer the tuna to a plate, cover with aluminum foil, and let rest for a few minutes. Serve with the salsa and plenty of fresh crusty bread.

4 tuna steaks (about 8 oz each)
1 tablespoon olive oil
2 tablespoons freshly crushed
  black peppercorns
1 teaspoon salt
lime wedges, to serve

Mango salsa
1 large mango, pitted and diced
½ red onion, finely chopped
1 large red chile, seeded and
  finely chopped
1 tablespoon lime juice
2 tablespoons chopped fresh
  cilantro
salt and black pepper

Serves **4**
Prep time **10 minutes,**
plus standing
Cooking time **2-4 minutes**

BLACKENED TUNA WITH MANGO SALSA

1 To make the mango salsa, mix together all the ingredients in a bowl and season with salt and black pepper. Let stand to let the flavors develop.

2 Brush the tuna steaks with a little oil and season with the peppercorns and salt. Cook on a grill rack over a hot barbecue grill or campfire for 1-2 minutes on each side, or until well seared on the outside but still pink in the middle. Alternatively, cook for a little less time, or for longer, until cooked to your preference.

3 Transfer the tuna to a plate, cover with aluminum foil, and let rest for a few minutes, then serve with the salsa and lime wedges for squeezing over the fish.

SWORDFISH STEAKS
WITH BASIL & PINE NUT OIL

1 teaspoon olive oil
4 swordfish steaks (about
   5 oz each)
1 (7 oz) package mixed
   leafy greens
½ cup drained and coarsely
   chopped sun-dried tomatoes
   in oil
salt and black pepper

Basil and pine nut oil
1 small bunch of basil, leaves
   stripped
5 teaspoons olive oil
1 tablespoon toasted pine nuts
1 tablespoon lemon juice

1 Brush the oil over the swordfish steaks and season well with salt and black pepper. Cook on a grill rack over a barbecue grill or campfire for 5-7 minutes, turning once, until nicely charred on the outside but still slightly pink in the middle.

2 Meanwhile, to make the basil oil, crush all the ingredients in a mortar and pestle, then season with salt and black pepper. Alternatively, finely chop the basil and pine nuts and mix together with the oil and lemon juice.

3 Pile the mixed leafy greens onto plates and sprinkle with the tomatoes. Transfer the swordfish to the plates and serve drizzled with a little basil oil.

Serves **4**
Prep time **15 minutes**
Cooking time **5-7 minutes**

Olive & Citrus Salmon

1 Remove any stray bones from the salmon fillets. Place the fish on 4 large pieces of heavy-duty aluminum foil and top each with one-quarter of the olives, tomatoes, oil, lemon, and honey. Season with salt and black pepper, then bring the foil up around the fish and seal well.

2 Cook the packages on a grill rack over a hot barbecue grill or campfire for 8-10 minutes, or until the fish is cooked through, then transfer to a plate and let rest for a few minutes.

3 Carefully open the packages, sprinkle with chopped parsley, and serve with tabbouleh.

4 salmon fillets (about 7 oz each)
12 large black ripe olives, pitted and halved
12 cherry tomatoes, halved
¼ cup olive oil
2 lemon wedges, thinly sliced
2 teaspoons honey
salt and black pepper
chopped parsley, to garnish
Tabbouleh (see page 208), to serve

Serves **4**
Prep time **5 minutes**
Cooking time **8-10 minutes**

Stuffed Salmon Fillets
WITH PANCETTA & TOMATOES

3 shallots, thinly sliced
3 garlic cloves, finely chopped
¾ cup drained and chopped
  sun-dried tomatoes in oil
3 tablespoons chopped
  tarragon
2 skinless salmon fillets
  (about 1 lb each)
6 thin pancetta or bacon slices
salt and black pepper

Serves 5-6
Prep time 15 minutes
Cooking time 40-60 minutes

1 Mix together the shallots, garlic, sun-dried tomatoes, tarragon, and a little salt and black pepper in a bowl.

2 Remove any stray bones from the salmon fillets. Place one fillet, skinned side up, on a board and spread the shallot mixture on top. Cover with the remaining salmon fillet, skinned side down. Space the pancetta or bacon slices across the salmon, tucking any long ends underneath. Tie kitchen string around the salmon to hold to the fillets together and secure the bacon slices in place.

3 Brush a grill rack with oil and place over a barbecue grill or campfire fire. Cook the salmon for 20-30 minutes on each side, or until cooked through, turning the fish over several times to check that it's not burning on the underside.

4 Transfer to a board or plate and cut away the string. Serve in chunky slices.

CAMPING TIP

If you have to take your tent down when it's blowing a gale, remove the poles first and leave the pegs until last. That way it won't end up turning into a giant parachute and flying off over the horizon.

MACKEREL
WITH *Citrus Fennel* SALAD

1 Slash each mackerel 3-4 times on each side with a sharp knife. Brush with a little oil and season inside and out with salt and black pepper. Using kitchen string, tie 3 lemon slices on each side of the fish.

2 Brush with a little more oil and cook on a grill rack over a hot barbecue grill or campfire for 4-5 minutes on each side, or until lightly charred and cooked through. Cover with aluminum foil and let rest for 5 minutes.

3 Toss together the fennel slices and feathery leaves, garlic, capers, oil, parsley, and lemon juice in a bowl, then season with salt and black pepper. Serve the mackerel with the fennel salad.

4 mackerel (about 12 oz each)
olive oil, for brushing
3 lemons, thinly sliced

Fennel salad
1 fennel bulb, trimmed and
   thinly sliced, feathery
   leaves reserved
1 small garlic clove, crushed
2 tablespoons capers,
   drained
2 tablespoons olive oil
1 tablespoon chopped parsley
2 tablespoons lemon juice
salt and black pepper

Serves **4**
Prep time **20 minutes**
Cooking time **8-10 minutes**

MACKEREL FILLETS
WITH *Pickled Beets*

2 fresh beets, grated
3 tablespoons finely
 chopped dill
2 shallots, finely chopped
2 teaspoons white wine vinegar
1 teaspoon sugar
4 small mackerel fillets
salt and black pepper
a pat of butter, cubed

Herb yogurt
¼ cup Greek yogurt
2 tablespoons finely chopped
 parsley
squeeze of lemon juice

Serves **2**
Prep time **15 minutes**
Cooking time **20-30 minutes**

1 Mix together the beets, dill, shallots, vinegar, sugar, and a little salt and black pepper in a bowl. Put 2 mackerel fillets on a board, skin side down, and spread the beet mixture on top. Place the remaining fillets, skin side up, on top to sandwich the filling.

2 Transfer the stuffed fillets to 2 large squares of heavy-duty aluminum foil and dot with the butter, then bring the foil up around the fish and seal well. Tuck between hot coals or logs to cook for 20-30 minutes, or until the mackerel is cooked through. Rotate the packages once or twice during cooking.

3 Meanwhile, beat the yogurt, parsley, lemon juice, and a little salt and black pepper in a bowl. Serve with the fish.

CHARGRILLED
SARDINES
with mango & lime salsa

1 Crush together the ginger, lime zest and juice, cilantro, oil, and chile in a mortar and pestle to make a coarse paste.

2 Score small slits into the sardine flesh, then rub the paste all over, massaging it into the slits.

3 Cook the sardines on a grill rack over a hot barbecue grill or campfire for 3-4 minutes on each side, or until cooked through and slightly blackened.

4 Meanwhile, to make the salsa, mix together all the ingredients in a small bowl. Serve with the sardines.

1 teaspoon peeled and finely grated fresh ginger root
finely grated zest and juice of 1 lime
1 small bunch of cilantro, coarsely chopped
1 tablespoon vegetable oil
½ large red chile, seeded and chopped
12-16 fresh sardines, scaled, gutted, and cleaned

Mango and lime salsa
1 firm, ripe mango, peeled, pitted, and diced
4 tomatoes, seeded and diced
1 scallion, finely chopped
2 tablespoons lime juice
½ large red chile, seeded and chopped

Serves 4
Prep time **20 minutes**
Cooking time **6-8 minutes**

SEASONED JUMBO SHRIMP
WITH BABY CORN & MANGO SALSA

1 Mix together the sea salt, Chinese 5-spice powder, and black, Sichuan, and cayenne peppers in a large bowl, then add the shrimp and toss until well coated in the spices.

2 Heat a ridged grill pan over a barbecue grill or campfire until hot, arrange the shrimp over the pan and cook for 4-5 minutes, or until the shrimp turn pink and are cooked through but still juicy.

3 Meanwhile, to make the baby corn and mango salsa, mix together the baby corn, scallions, red chile, and diced mango in a bowl, then stir in the sweet soy sauce.

4 Serve the shrimp with the baby corn and mango salsa along with the tortillas (and a large bowl for the shells).

1 teaspoon coarse sea salt
1 teaspoon Chinese 5-spice powder
1 teaspoon cracked black pepper
½ teaspoon Sichuan peppercorns, crushed
pinch of cayenne pepper
1 lb raw jumbo shrimp, with shells on, rinsed
8 soft flour tortillas, to serve

Baby corn and mango salsa
14 baby corn, sliced into circles
2 scallions, trimmed and finely chopped
1 chile, seeded and finely chopped
1 small mango, peeled, pitted and diced
2 tablespoons sweet soy sauce (ketjap manis)

Serves **4**
Prep time **15 minutes**
Cooking time **about 5 minutes**

SHRIMP
with PIRI PIRI

1 Mix together the oil, lemon zest and juice, piri piri seasoning, tomato paste, garlic, and salt and black pepper in a bowl. Add the shrimp and toss until evenly coated. Cover with plastic wrap and let marinate in a cooler for at least 2 hours.

2 Thread the shrimp onto 12 metal skewers through the thickest part of the body and tail. Transfer to a grill rack over a hot barbecue grill or campfire and cook for 5-6 minutes, turning once, until the shrimp turn pink and cooked through.

3 Sprinkle the shrimp with chopped parsley and serve with lemon wedges for squeezing over them.

3 tablespoons olive oil
grated zest and juice of 1 lemon
2 teaspoons piri piri seasoning
2 teaspoons tomato paste
2 garlic cloves, finely chopped
12 oz raw jumbo shrimp, shells
  on and heads removed, rinsed
salt and black pepper
chopped parsley, to garnish
lemon wedges, to serve

Serves **6**
Prep time **15 minutes,**
plus marinating
Cooking time **5-6 minutes**

CAMPING TIP

If you're planning on having an alcoholic drink while you camp, make sure you bring screw-top bottles of wine and ring-pull cans of beer. Corkscrews and bottle openers tend to go astray and are particularly hard to find after dark when the drinking begins in earnest.

GRILLED SARDINES
with tomato salsa

3 fresh sardines (about 4 oz, scaled, gutted, and cleaned
¼ cup lemon juice
2 slices of ciabatta bread
salt and black pepper
1 tablespoon chopped basil, to garnish

Tomato salsa
8 cherry tomatoes, chopped
1 scallion, sliced
1 tablespoon chopped basil
½ red bell pepper, cored, seeded, and chopped

Serves 1
Prep time **10 minutes**
Cooking time **6-8 minutes**

1 To make the tomato salsa, mix together all the ingredients in a bowl.

2 Place the sardines on a plate, drizzle with the lemon juice, and season with salt and black pepper. Transfer to a grill rack over a hot barbecue grill or campfire and cook for 3-4 minutes on each side or until cooked through.

3 Meanwhile, toast the bread on the rack until lightly charred.

4 Sprinkle the sardines with the chopped basil and serve immediately with the tomato salsa and toasted ciabatta.

ALL ABOUT THE
CAMPFIRE

Our love affair with campfires began the day cave dwellers discovered that rubbing two sticks together for long enough produced fire (along with a fistful of blisters). Since then, this method for keeping warm, scaring off wild beasts, and turning unpalatable raw meat into something tasty and safe for consumption has been a global hit. Modern man has wholeheartedly adopted this cooking technique—in the form of the barbecue—to bond with nature and exert his masculinity ... with modern woman standing close by with a fire pail and a plate of extra steaks.

Camping offers the ideal opportunity to explore your hunter-gatherer alter ego and get back to basics. The campfire is the heart of the camping experience, drawing people together to socialize, enjoy the warmth, and sizzle a frankfurter or two.

LIGHTING THE FIRE

If your campsite site sells wood, buy some—it will probably be dried out and ready to burn, instead of the collection of damp branches you'll find if you go out gathering your own. You'll need some small twigs, grass, or newspaper to get the fire going and you should make a pile of this in the center, then build up a tentlike structure of bigger kindling and logs around it. Light the kindling and (hopefully) watch as your campfire comes to life.

A FIRE FOR ALL OCCASIONS

If your fire is purely an atmospheric addition to the evening, then you can keep adding logs to fuel the flames. However, a cooking fire requires the logs to burn down into charcoal so the heat is even and hot enough to cook food (see page 8 for campfire cooking techniques).

PUTTING OUT THE FIRE

When the last of the wine has been consumed and it's time to call it a night and crawl into your tent, you need to be meticulous about putting out the campfire. You should gradually let the wood burn down about half an hour before you anticipate the end of the evening. Once the flames have disappeared, you should sprinkle a little water all over the embers and spread them out so that you can make sure the fire has completely extinguished.

POTATO & CHEESE CAKES

6 red skinned potatoes
(about 1½ lb), unpeeled
1¾ cups shredded mild cheddar
or American cheese
1 red onion, finely chopped
2 tablespoons butter
salt and black pepper

To serve (optional)
smoked trout fillets
cucumber slices

Serves **6**
Prep time **10 minutes,
plus cooling**
Cooking time **30 minutes**

1 Cook the potatoes in a large saucepan of boiling water
for about 20 minutes, or until just cooked but firm. Drain
and let cool.

2 Peel the potatoes and grate them into a bowl. Stir in
the shredded cheese and chopped onion and season
with salt and black pepper. Divide the mixture into 6 and
shape into circles, using wet hands, then press down with
two fingers to form flattened cakes. Tidy up the edges.

3 Melt half the butter in a ridged grill pan or skillet over
a barbecue grill or campfire, add half the cakes, and
cook for about 5 minutes, turning once, until golden brown
and heated through. Transfer to a plate, then repeat with the
remaining butter and cakes.

4 Serve the cakes warm or cold, with lightly smoked
trout fillets and cucumber slices, if desired.

Cheddar
BURGERS
WITH CUCUMBER SALSA

1 cup drained lima beans,
   drained
1 onion, finely chopped
1 carrot, shredded
1 cup shredded sharp
   cheddar cheese
2 cups fresh bread crumbs
1 egg
1 teaspoon cumin seeds
vegetable oil, for frying
4 round rolls
salt and black pepper

Cucumber salsa
½ small cucumber
2 tablespoons chopped
   fresh cilantro
2 scallions, finely chopped
1 tablespoon lemon or lime juice
1 teaspoon sugar

Serves 4
Prep time **15 minutes**
Cooking time **8 minutes**

1 Put the lima beans into a bowl and lightly mash with a fork. Add the onion, carrot, cheese, bread crumbs, egg, cumin seeds, and salt and black pepper and mix until evenly combined.

2 Divide the mixture into 4 and shape into small flat cakes. Heat a little oil in a ridged grill pan or skillet over a barbecue grill or campfire and cook the patties for about 8 minutes, turning once, until crisp, golden, and heated through.

3 Meanwhile, for the salsa, halve the cucumber, scoop out the seeds, and finely chop. Toss in a bowl with the cilantro, scallions, lemon or lime juice, sugar, and a little salt and black pepper.

4 Split the rolls and fill with the burgers and salsa.

MUSHROOM, COUSCOUS,
& HERB SAUSAGES

• •

1 Put the couscous into a heatproof bowl and add ⅓ cup of boiling water. Cover with plastic wrap and let stand for 5 minutes, then fluff up with a fork.

2 Meanwhile, heat the olive oil in a skillet, add the onion, mushrooms, and chile, and sauté over high heat for about 5 minutes, until the mushrooms are golden and the moisture has evaporated.

3 Turn into a bowl, add the remaining ingredients and couscous, and mix well. Divide the mixture into 12 and shape into cylindrical shapes, using lightly floured hands. Cover with plastic wrap and chill in a cooler for 30 minutes.

4 Brush the sausages with a little oil and cook on a grill rack over a barbecue grill or campfire for about 10 minutes, turning frequently, until golden and piping hot in the middle.

⅓ cup couscous
3 tablespoons olive oil,
  plus extra for brushing
1 onion, finely chopped
4 cups finely chopped
  cremini mushrooms
1 red chile, seeded and
  finely sliced
3 garlic cloves, finely chopped
small handful of mixed herbs,
  such as thyme, rosemary, and
  parsley, finely chopped
12 whole cooked chestnuts,
  finely chopped
¾ cup fresh bread crumbs
1 egg yolk
flour, for dusting
salt and black pepper

Serves **4**
Prep time **15 minutes,**
plus chilling
Cooking time **10 minutes**

TOMATO, PESTO, & OLIVE *Pizzas*

2 cups white bread flour,
  plus extra for dusting
½ teaspoon salt
1 teaspoon active dry yeast
1 tablespoon olive oil, plus extra
  for brushing and drizzling

Topping
2 tablespoons r pesto
12 cherry tomatoes, halved
5 oz mozzarella cheese, sliced
¼ cup pitted black ripe olives,
  halved
handful of basil leaves
salt and black pepper

Serves **2**
Prep time **30 minutes,
plus rising**
Cooking time **20-24 minutes**

1 To make the pizza crust, mix the flour, salt, and yeast in a
bowl. Make a well in the center, add ½ cup of lukewarm water
and the oil, and mix with a blunt knife until the mixture comes
together into a ball. Turn out onto a floured board and knead
for about 10 minutes, until the dough is smooth and elastic. (If
you've no surface to work on, work the dough in the bowl as
best as you can.) Return the dough to the bowl, cover with a
clean dish towel or plastic wrap, and let rest in a warm place
(near the fire if already lit) until doubled in size.

2 Punch the dough to deflate it, then cut in half. Roll out
a piece on a floured board to a circle about 9 inches in
diameter. Lightly brush a heavy skillet with oil and press the
dough into the bottom. Spread half the pesto over the dough
and top with half the tomatoes, mozzarella, and olives, some
salt and black pepper, and a drizzle more oil.

3 Place the pan on a grill rack over a moderately hot
barbecue grill or campfire, make a dome of aluminum
foil, and position over the pizza, tucking the ends under the
bottom to secure. Cook for 10-12 minutes, until the crust
is crisp underneath and the cheese melted. Carefully slide
the pizza out onto a board, sprinkle with half the basil leaves,
and serve hot. Repeat with the remaining ingredients to make
the second pizza.

DOUBLE CHEESE *Margherita* PIZZA

2 cups white bread flour, plus
    extra for dusting
1 teaspoon active dry yeast
1 teaspoon salt
2 tablespoons olive oil

Topping
1 cup can diced tomatoes
2 tablespoons sun-dried
    tomato paste
1 teaspoon sugar
1 small garlic clove, crushed
8 oz mozzarella cheese, thinly
    sliced
1 cup grated Parmesan cheese
handful of pitted
    black ripe olives
salt and black pepper

Serves **4**
Prep time **25 minutes,
plus rising**
Cooking time **about
30 minutes**

1 To make the pizza crust, mix the flour, yeast, salt, and olive oil in a bowl and add ³⁄₄ cup lukewarm water. Mix with a blunt knife to make a soft dough, adding a dash more water if the dough feels dry. Turn out onto a floured board and knead for about 10 minutes, until the dough is smooth and elastic. (If you've no surface to work on, work the dough in the bowl as best as you can.) Return the dough to the bowl, cover with a clean dish towel or plastic wrap, and let rest in a warm place (near the fire if already lit) until doubled in size.

2 Heat a sturdy baking sheet on a rack over the fire while assembling the pizza. Turn the dough out onto a floured board and roll out to a circle about 12 inches in diameter. Transfer to the baking sheet.

3 Mix together the tomatoes, tomato paste, sugar, garlic, and a little salt and black pepper and spread over the crust to about ½ inch from the edges. Arrange the mozzarella slices on top and sprinkle with the Parmesan. Sprinkle with the olives and season with salt and black pepper. Make a dome of aluminum foil and position over the pizza, tucking the ends under the bottom to secure. Cook for about 30 minutes, or until the crust is cooked and the cheese is melting.

COOKING TIP
You can add your favorite toppings to the basic pizza above. Try a sprinkling of capers, chopped anchovies, fresh herbs, cherry tomatoes, chopped artichokes, sliced pepperoni, or diced crispy bacon. Chargrilled vegetables, such as bell peppers, zucchini, eggplants, mushrooms, and asparagus (cooked on over a barbecue grill or campfire before the pizza) are also delicious.

INDIAN SPICED
SWEET POTATOES

1 Cut the potatoes across into ½ inch thick slices and put into the centers of 4 large squares of heavy-duty aluminum foil.

2 Mix together the coconut, cardamom, garlic, chile, and 2 tablespoons of the cilantro in a bowl. Spoon the mixture over the potatoes and drizzle with the oil. Bring the foil up around the filling and seal well.

3 Tuck the packages between hot coals or logs to cook. This will take 1-2 hours, depending on the intensity of the fire. Rotate the package several times during cooking so the potatoes cook evenly.

4 Carefully open the packages and serve sprinkled with the remaining cilantro.

3 large sweet potatoes
   (about 1½ lb), scrubbed
⅓ cup unsweetened
   dry coconut
8 cardamom pods, crushed to
   release the seeds
2 garlic cloves, finely chopped
1 small hot chile, seeded and
   finely chopped
3 tablespoons chopped
   fresh cilantro
2 tablespoons vegetable oil
salt

Serves **4**
Prep time **15 minutes**
Cooking time **1-2 hours**

ONE DISH

STEAK & ALE CASSEROLE

VEGETABLE & TOFU
STIR-FRY

COCONUT DHAL & TOASTED
NAAN STRIPS

BEEF, PUMPKIN & GINGER STEW

2 tablespoons all-purpose flour
1½ lb boneless beef chuck or
  beef round, diced
2 tablespoons butter
3 tablespoons olive oil
1 onion, chopped
2 carrots, sliced
2 parsnips, sliced
3 bay leaves
several thyme sprigs
2 tablespoons tomato paste
5 cups peeled and seeded
  small pumpkin chunks
1 tablespoon packed dark
  brown sugar
½ cup fresh ginger root,
  peeled and finely chopped
small handful of parsley,
  chopped, plus extra to garnish
salt and black pepper

Serves **6**
Prep time **20 minutes**
Cooking time 1½ **hours**

1 Put the flour on a plate and season with salt and black
  pepper, then coat the beef in the flour. Heat the butter
and oil in a large saucepan and sauté the meat, in two batches,
until browned, then transfer the browned meat to a plate with
a slotted spoon.

2 Add the onion, carrots, and parsnips to the saucepan
  and cook gently for 5 minutes. Return the meat to the
pan and add the herbs and tomato paste. Add just enough water
to cover the ingredients and bring slowly to a boil. Cover with
a lid and cook over low heat, simmering gently for 45 minutes.

3 Add the pumpkin, sugar, ginge,r and parsley, replace the
  lid, and cook for another 30 minutes, or until the pumpkin
is soft and the meat is tender. Adjust the seasoning, if necessary,
and serve sprinkled with extra parsley.

QUICK CHILI
TACOS

1 Heat the oil in a large saucepan, add the onion and garlic, and cook over medium heat for about 5 minutes, until softened. Add the ground beef and sauté for another 5 minutes, breaking it up with a wooden spoon, until browned.

2 Stir in the tomato puree or sauce, beans, chili sauce, and salt and black pepper to taste and bring to a boil. Cover with a lid and simmer over medium-low heat for 15 minutes, stirring occasionally, until thickened.

3 Spoon the chili onto the tortillas and serve with the cheese, sour cream, and cilantro.

2 tablespoons olive oil
1 large onion, finely chopped
2 garlic cloves, crushed
1 lb ground minced beef
1 (24-28 oz) can or jar tomato puree or tomato sauce
1 (15 oz) can red kidney beans, drained
2-3 tablespoons hot chili sauce
salt and black pepper

To serve
8 soft corn tortillas, warmed
1 cup shredded cheddar cheese
½ cup sour cream
handful of fresh cilantro sprigs

Serves **4**
Prep time **5 minutes**
Cooking time **30 minutes**

COOKING TIP

To warm tortillas, pita breads, and naans, place on a grill rack over a hot barbecue grill or campfire, or in a skillet over high heat, for 30–60 seconds on each side.

Easy Campfire
BEEF CHILI

1 tablespoon vegetable oil
1 large onion, chopped
1 lb ground beef
1 (14 ½ oz) can diced tomatoes
¼ cup sweet chili sauce
1 tablespoon ground paprika
1 (15 oz) can red kidney beans,
    drained
squeeze of lemon juice
salt and black pepper

To serve
1 small avocado
1 small tomato, finely diced
sour cream
Garlic Bread (see page 206)

Serves **4**
Prep time **15 minutes**
Cooking time **about**
1¼ **hours**

1 Heat the oil in a large saucepan. Add the onion and cook for about 5 minutes, until softened. Add the ground beef and sauté for another 5-10 minutes, breaking it up with a wooden spoon, until lightly browned.

2 Add the canned tomatoes, 3 tablespoons of the chili sauce, and the paprika and heat until simmering. Cover with a lid and cook gently for 20-30 minutes, until thick and pulpy. Stir in the kidney beans and lemon juice and cook for another 15 minutes, until heated through.

3 Meanwhile, to make a simple salsa, peel, pit, and finely dice the avocado. Put in a bowl with the tomato and remaining chili sauce and mix together.

4 Serve the chili with sour cream, salsa, and garlic bread.

STEAK & ALE *Casserole*

2 tablespoons all-purpose flour
2 lb chuck shoulder steak
  or chuck blade steak,
  cut into chunks
2 tablespoons butter
1 tablespoon olive oil
2 onions, chopped
2 celery sticks, sliced
several thyme sprigs
2 bay leaves
1¾ cups strong ale
1¼ cups beef stock or broth
2 tablespoons molasses
4 parsnips (about 1 lb),
  cut into wedges
salt and black pepper
crusty bread, to serve

Serves **5-6**
Prep time **20 minutes**
Cooking time **1¾ hours**

1 Put the flour onto a plate and season with salt and black pepper, then coat the beef in the flour. Heat the butter and oil in a large saucepan and sauté the beef, in batches, until deep brown, then transfer the browned meat to a plate with a slotted spoon.

2 Add the onions and celery to the pan and sauté for about 5 minutes, until softened. Return the beef to the pan and add the herbs, ale, stock or broth, and molasses. Bring just to a boil, then cover with a lid and simmer gently for 1 hour.

3 Add the parsnips to the pan, replace the lid, and cook for another 30 minutes, or until the beef and parsnips are tender. Adjust the seasoning, if necessary, and serve with crusty bread.

SPICED BEEF & ONION
CHAPPATIS

1 Put the beef, sliced onion, spices, and 1 tablespoon of the oil into a bowl and toss well to coat, then season with salt and black pepper.

2 Heat the remaining oil in a skillet, add the red onion wedges, and cook over medium heat for 2-3 minutes, or until softened. Add the beef and sliced onion and cook for 1-2 minutes on each side, or until golden and cooked through.

3 Spoon the beef and onions onto one side of each chapatti, top with the lime pickle and leafy greens, then fold over to enclose the filling and serve.

10 oz thinly cut sirloin, tri-tip, or
   flank steak, thinly sliced
1 small onion, thinly sliced
1 teaspoon ground cumin
½ teaspoon ground paprika
½ teaspoon ground coriander
2 tablespoons olive oil
1 red onion, cut into thin wedges
2 soft wheat chapattis, warmed
2 tablespoons lime pickle
2 handfuls of mixed leafy
   greens, such as argula, mâche,
   or mizuna
salt and black pepper

Serves **2**
Prep time **10 minutes**
Cooking time **about 10 minutes**

CAMPING TIP

If you're cooking over a fire, make sure your campsite allows campfires. There may be assigned spots for setting fire to sticks, or you might have a fire pit or barbecue area next to your pitch. It might seem obvious, but make sure there's plenty of clear space around the fire.

CLASSIC LIVER & *Bacon*

CALF LIVER IS THE TRADITIONAL CHOICE FOR PAN-FRYING WITH BACON, BUT YOU COULD USE LAMB LIVER AS A SUBSTITUTE, IF AVAILABLE FROM YOUR BUTCHER. COOK THE LIVER A LITTLE LONGER, IF YOU PREFER IT COOKED THROUGH BUT BE CAREFUL NOT TO COOK IT FOR TOO LONG OR IT WILL START TO TOUGHEN UP.

all-purpose flour, to coat
1¼ lb liver
2 tablespoons butter
1 tablespoon olive oil
12 large sage leaves
8 bacon slices
⅔ cup hard dry cider
salt and black pepper

Serves 4
Prep time **10 minutes**
Cooking time **about 10 minutes**

1 Put the flour on a plate and season with salt and black pepper. Cut away any tubes from the liver, then dust it with the flour.

2 Heat half the butter with the oil in a skillet until foaming. Add the sage leaves and cook for about 30 seconds, until sizzling. Using a slotted spoon, transfer to a plate lined with paper towels.

3 Add the bacon to the pan and cook until golden, then transfer to the plate, cover with aluminum foil, and keep warm.

4 Add the liver to the pan and cook for about 2 minutes, until deep golden. Turn the slices over and return the bacon and sage to the pan. Cook for another 1-2 minutes, until still slightly pink in the middle, or until cooked to your preference. Transfer to a plate, cover with foil, and keep warm.

5 Add the cider to the pan and let it simmer until slightly reduced, scraping up any residue. Whisk in the remaining butter and adjust the seasoning, if necessary. Serve the liver and bacon with the sauce spooned over them and sprinkled with the sage leaves.

LIVER WITH LEEKS
& *Cannellini Beans*

¼ cup all-purpose flour
4 pieces liver (about 4 oz each)
4 teaspoons olive oil
4 large leeks, trimmed
   and sliced
4 lean bacon slices, chopped
1 (15 oz) can cannellini beans,
   drained
¼ cup crème fraîche or
   sour cream
salt and black pepper
chopped parsley or thyme,
   to garnish

Serves 4
Prep time 10 minutes
Cooking time 10 minutes

1 Put the flour onto a plate and season with salt and black pepper, then coat the liver in the flour.

2 Heat half the oil in a skillet, add the liver, and cook for about 2 minutes on each side, until still slightly pink in the middle, or until cooked to your preference. Transfer to a plate, cover with aluminum foil, and keep warm.

3 Heat the remaining oil in the skillet, add the leeks and bacon, and cook for 3-4 minutes, or until the leeks are softened and the bacon is cooked through. Stir in the cannellini beans and crème fraîche or sour cream, season with black pepper, and heat through.

4 Serve the liver with the beans, sprinkled with chopped parsley or thyme.

Rose-Scented LAMB
WITH EGGPLANTS

1 Heat 3 tablespoons of the oil in a large saucepan, add the eggplants, and cook for about 10 minutes, stirring frequently, until browned. Transfer to a plate.

2 Heat the remaining oil in the pan and cook the lamb, in batches, until browned, then transfer the browned meat to a plate with a slotted spoon. Return all the meat to the pan, add the onions, and sauté for another 5 minutes. Add the garlic and spices and sauté for another 2 minutes.

3 Stir in the ginger, tomatoes, and stock or broth and bring to a gentle simmer. Cover with a lid or aluminum foil and cook for about 1 hour, or until the lamb is tender. Stir in the eggplants, dates, and rose water and cook for another 20 minutes, stirring occasionally, until the eggplants are tender.

4 Once the lamb is almost ready, put the couscous into a heatproof bowl and pour 1¾ cups of boiling water over the grains. Cover with plastic wrap and let stand for 5 minutes, then fluff up with a fork.

5 Season the lamb with salt and black pepper and add a little hot water, if necessary. Serve with the couscous.

⅓ cup olive oil
2 eggplants, diced
2 lb lean shoulder of lamb, excess fat removed and cut into small chunks
2 onions, chopped
3 garlic cloves, chopped
1 teaspoon each of ground turmeric, cinnamon, cumin, and coriander
½ teaspoon ground cloves
½ inch piece of fresh ginger root, peeled and finely chopped
1 (14½ oz) can diced tomatoes
1¼ cups hot lamb or chicken stock or broth
5 pitted dates, coarsely chopped
1 teaspoon rose water
2 cups couscous
salt and black pepper

Serves 6
Prep time **20 minutes**
Cooking time **about 1¾ hours**

SAUSAGE &
Sweet Potato Hash

3 tablespoons olive oil
8 pork link sausages
3 large red onions, thinly sliced
1 teaspoon sugar
3 sweet potatoes (about 1 lb),
   scrubbed and cut into small
   chunks
8 sage leaves
2 tablespoons balsamic vinegar
salt and black pepper

Serves **4**
Prep time **15 minutes**
Cooking time **45 minutes**

1 Heat the oil in a skillet, add the sausages, and cook for about 10 minutes, turning frequently, until browned. Transfer to a plate.

2 Add the onions and sugar to the pan and cook gently, stirring frequently, until lightly browned. Return the sausages to the pan with the sweet potatoes, sage leaves, and a little salt and black pepper.

3 Cover the pan with a lid or aluminum foil and cook over gentle heat for about 25 minutes, or until the potatoes are tender and the sausages are cooked through. Drizzle with the vinegar and adjust the seasoning, if necessary, before serving.

SPICY SAUSAGE
& Arugula Pasta

2 tablespoons olive oil
8 Italian-style sausages, skins
  removed
1¾ cups tomato puree or
  tomato sauce
1 teaspoon dried red
  pepper flakes
4 handfuls of arugula
salt and black pepper

To serve
cooked penne or other pasta
  (see page 10)
grated Parmesan cheese

Serves **4**
Prep time **10 minutes**
Cooking time **15 minutes**

1 Heat the oil in a skillet, break the sausages into small pieces and add to the pan, then cook for about 5 minutes, turning occasionally, until browned.

2 Add the tomato puree or sauce and dried red pepper flakes and season with salt and black pepper. Cover with a lid and bring to a boil, then simmer gently for about 5 minutes, or until the sauce is slightly reduced and the sausages are cooked through.

3 Add the pasta to the sauce, toss well to coat, and heat through. Remove from the heat, stir in the arugula, and serve with grated Parmesan.

EASY CASSOULET

2 tablespoons olive oil
4 good-quality link sausages
4 boneless, skinless chicken
  thighs, opened out flat
1 large onion, chopped
2 celery sticks, chopped
2 teaspoons smoked paprika
2 (14½ oz) cans diced tomatoes
  with garlic and herbs
2 (15 oz) cans cannellini beans,
  drained
2 tablespoons chopped parsley
salt and black pepper

1 Heat the oil in a large saucepan, add the sausages and chicken thighs, and cook for about 5 minutes, turning occasionally, until browned. Remove the meat from the pan and slice the sausages.

2 Add the onion and celery to the pan and sauté for 2–3 minutes, until slightly softened. Add the paprika, stir well, and return the sausages and chicken to the pan.

3 Add the tomatoes and beans and season with salt and black pepper. Bring to a boil, then cover with a lid and simmer gently for about 20 minutes, or until the meat is cooked through. Serve sprinkled with the parsley.

Serves **4**
Prep time **15 minutes**
Cooking time **30 minutes**

COOKING TIP

For an authentic cassoulet, sauté
½ cup fresh white bread crumbs in
1 tablespoon olive oil until golden
and serve the cooked dish
sprinkled with the fried
bread crumbs.

CAMPFIRE
PORK GOULASH
with Caraway Dumplings

2 tablespoons vegetable oil
2 lb lean pork, diced
2 onions, sliced
1 tablespoon paprika
¼ cup tomato paste
3 cups hot pork or chicken stock
   or broth
3 tablespoons packed light
   brown sugar
2 tablespoons red wine vinegar
½ red cabbage, shredded
salt and black pepper

Dumplings
1¼ cups all-purpose flour
1 teaspoon baking powder
⅓ cup beef suet or vegetable
   shortening
1 teaspoon caraway seeds

Serves **6**
Prep time **20 minutes**
Cooking time **1¾-2 hours**

1 Heat a large saucepan. Add the oil and cook the pork, in batches, until browned, then transfer the browned meat to a plate with a slotted spoon. Return all the meat to the pan with the onions and sauté, stirring, for 5 minutes.

2 Add the paprika, tomato paste, stock or broth, sugar, and vinegar to the pan and bring to a simmer. Cover with a lid and cook gently for 1-1¼ hours, until the meat is tender, stirring frequently.

3 Add the cabbage to the pan and cook for another 20 minutes, until tender.

4 Meanwhile, mix the flour, baking powder, suet or shortening, and caraway seeds in a bowl and season lightly with salt and black pepper. Stir in enough cold water to make a thick, sticky paste.

5 Stir a little hot water into the goulash if it has dried out. (It should be really wet, because the dumplings will absorb some of the stock.) Place tablespoonfuls of the dumpling mixture over the goulash. Cover with the lid and cook for another 10-15 minutes, until the dumplings are light and fluffy.

CHORIZO WITH LENTILS
& Red Wine

1 Heat the oil in a skillet, add the chorizo, and cook for 1–2 minutes on each side, until golden and the natural oil is released. Transfer to a plate.

2 Add the onion to the pan and sauté over medium heat for about 5 minutes, until softened. Stir in the lentils and wine, bring to a simmer, and cook for a few minutes.

3 Pour in the stock or broth, return the chorizo to the pan, and simmer for about 25 minutes, or until most of the liquid is absorbed and the lentils are tender. Sprinkle with chopped parsley and serve with plenty of bread.

1 tablespoon olive oil
8 oz chorizo sausage,
  thickly sliced
1 finely chopped onion
3/4 cup dried green lentils
1/2 cup fruity red wine
2 cups hot chicken stock or broth
chopped parsley, to garnish
crusty bread, to serve

Serves 4
Prep time **10 minutes**
Cooking time **about 40 minutes**

CHUNKY CHORIZO,
Pasta, & Bean Soup

THIS SUBSTANTIAL SOUP IS BASED ON THE ITALIAN CLASSIC, PASTA E FAGIOLI—
"PASTA AND BEANS," IN ENGLISH.

¼ cup olive oil
1 large onion, chopped
2 oz chorizo sausage, chopped
4 garlic cloves, crushed
2 tablespoons chopped thyme
5 cups tomato puree or
  tomato sauce
3 cups hot chicken stock
  or broth
2 (15 oz) cans cranberry beans,
  drained
8 oz small dried pasta shapes,
  such as conchigliette
3 tablespoons chopped basil
salt and black pepper
grated Parmesan cheese,
  to serve

Serves 4
Prep time 10 minutes
Cooking time 40 minutes

1 Heat the oil in a saucepan, add the onion, chorizo, garlic, and thyme, and sauté for about 5 minutes, or until the onion is softened and the chorizo is golden.

2 Add the tomato puree or sauce, stock or broth, cranberry beans, and salt and black pepper to the pan. Bring to a boil, then cover with a lid and simmer gently for 20 minutes.

3 Stir in the pasta shapes and basil and cook for another 8–10 minutes, or until the pasta is tender. Adjust the seasoning, if necessary, spoon into bowls, and serve topped with grated Parmesan.

CHORIZO HASH
WITH ZUCCHINI, POTATOES, & EGGS

2 tablespoons olive oil
4 red-skinned or white round
 potatoes (about 1 lb), diced
2 red onions, chopped
4 oz chorizo or blood sausages,
 cut into small dice
2 zucchini, cut into small dice
10 cherry tomatoes, halved
4 eggs
salt and black pepper

Serves 4
Prep time **20 minutes**
Cooking time **about
45 minutes**

1 Heat the oil in a skillet, add the potatoes, and cook over medium heat for 15 minutes, or until softened and beginning to brown.

2 Add the onions, sausage, and zucchini and cook for another 15 minutes, stirring frequently, until the ingredients are soft and lightly browned. Stir in the tomatoes and a little salt and black pepper.

3 Spread the ingredients in an even layer and make 4 indentations in the mixture. Break an egg into each and continue to cook for 15 minutes, or until the eggs are lightly set.

COOKING TIP

You can speed up the cooking time by covering the pan with a lid or aluminum foil, or by spooning the diced ingredients over the eggs once they start to turn opaque.

Fire-It-Up RISOTTO

1 Heat half the oil in a large saucepan, add the bacon, and cook, stirring, until crisp. Transfer to a plate.

2 Add the remaining oil and onion to the pan and cook, stirring, for about 5 minutes, adding the garlic once the onion is softened.

3 Stir the rice into the pan and pour in about 2/3 cup of the stock. Cook, stirring, until the stock is absorbed. Pour in a little more stock and cook again, stirring as the rice starts to swell. Continue to add the stock, stirring frequently, until the rice is just tender. If the risotto is too dry, add extra boiling water as necessary.

4 Stir in the bacon, beans, and cheese, season with a little salt and black pepper, and heat through. Stir in the arugula or spinach and serve once they've wilted and the beans are tender.

2 tablespoons olive oil
4 oz bacon, chopped
1 large onion, chopped
2 garlic cloves, finely chopped
1 3/4 cups risotto rice
4 cups hot chicken or vegetable stock (made with 2 bouillon cubes) or broth
1 cup fresh baby fava beans
1 cup shredded cheddar cheese
handful of arugula or fresh baby spinach
salt and black pepper

Serves 4
Prep time 15 minutes
Cooking time about 40 minutes

FIRST AID & SAFETY

Camping is generally a fairly safe vacation choice, but if you go unprepared or aren't aware of the safety risks, you could end up cutting your trip short with a trip to the hospital.

FIRST AID

Always check your first aid kit before you leave home and make sure everyone in your party knows where it's kept. If you take prescription medicine, make sure you have ample supplies to last while you're away and keep a note of the closest medical facilities and pharmacy. The most common injuries to occur will be stings, insect bites, cuts, or sprains, so include plenty of bandages, antiseptic cream, and sting relief in your first aid kit.

CAMPSITE HAZARDS

Fire is one of the biggest hazards on a campsite, which is why it's so important to choose a safe spot for your campfire—far away from your own and other people's tents, and away from trees and any other combustible materials. Always make sure your campfire is fully extinguished before you leave it (see page 83) and never leave children alone by a campfire.

TRIPS AND FALLS

Tent pegs and guy ropes can be the cause of many a twisted ankle, particularly at nighttime, when it's more difficult to see the ropes and to judge distances. When you're walking around the site at night, keep well clear of the tents and always carry a flashlight to check for any other obstacles that might be blocking your path.

CHILDREN

Camping offers kids a huge amount of freedom, but it's important to make them aware of potential dangers as well. Always set limits on how far they can roam away from the tent and about staying together when they do. Some campsites offer wristbands for kids, which you can write a contact number on in case they get lost. Another option is a set of walkie-talkies—these could also come in handy for treasure hunts and spy games.

SUN SAFETY

There doesn't have to be blazing sunshine to get sunburned—in fact, you're more probable to be caught unawares on a cloudy day when you're less fastidious about sun protection. Cover up during the heat of the day and wear sun hats if you're going for a hike or spending a lot of time outdoors.

Chicken
WITH ONION, LEMON, & ANCHOVIES

¼ cup olive oil
1 lemon, cut into wedges
12 boneless, skinless chicken
   thighs, each cut in half
4 onions, thinly sliced
½ teaspoon sugar
2 garlic cloves, chopped
½ cup dry white wine
⅔ cup hot chicken stock or
   broth
1 (2 oz) can anchovy fillets,
   chopped
handful of parsley, chopped
salt and black pepper

Serves 6
Prep time **20 minutes**
Cooking time **about 1¼ hours**

1 Heat 1 tablespoon of the oil in a large saucepan, add the lemon wedges, and brown lightly on the cut sides, then transfer to a plate.

2 Heat another 1 tablespoon of the oil in the pan, add the chicken, and brown lightly on all sides. Transfer to a plate.

3 Add the remaining oil to the pan, add the onions and sugar, and sauté gently for about 15 minutes or until the onions are soft and deep golden. Stir in the garlic and cook for another 1 minute.

4 Return the chicken to the pan with the wine, stock or broth, and anchovy fillets and bring to a simmer. Cover with a lid and cook gently for 45 minutes, or until the chicken is tender and cooked through, stirring frequently to stop the bottom of the pan from burning. Season with salt and black pepper and stir in the parsley to serve.

PAN-FRIED
CHICKEN LIVERS
WITH FENNEL

1 Put the flour onto a plate and season with a little salt and black pepper, then coat the chicken livers in the flour.

2 Heat the oil in a skillet and sauté the sliced fennel over medium-high heat for 3 minutes. Add the liver to the pan and cook for 5–8 minutes, stirring gently, until the liver is cooked to your preference.

3 Slowly stir in the parsley. Pour in the lemon juice, which will make a sizzling sound, then serve with some leafy greens.

1 tablespoon all-purpose flour
8 oz chicken livers, trimmed
2 teaspoons olive oil
1 fennel bulb and leaves, trimmed and sliced
3 tablespoons chopped flat leaf parsley
2 tablespoons lemon juice
salt and black pepper
leafy greens, such as argula, mâche, or mizuna, to serve

Serves **4**
Prep time **10 minutes**
Cooking time **10-12 minutes**

CHERRY TOMATO & COD STIR-FRY WITH BACON

1 Heat the oil in a skillet, add the scallions, garlic, and bacon, and cook over high heat for about 3 minutes, stirring frequently, until the onions are softened and the bacon is browned.

2 Add the tomatoes and fish and cook over medium heat for 3-4 minutes, or until the fish is opaque and cooked through, stirring gently and tossing occasionally so that the fish cubes stay intact as much as possible.

3 Sprinkle with the lemon zest and spinach, cover with a lid, and cook for about 2 minutes, until the spinach has wilted, then gently fold the ingredients together.

4 Sprinkle with the feta and serve with crusty bread to mop up the juices

2 tablespoons olive oil
1 bunch of scallions, trimmed
   and coarsely chopped
1 garlic clove, thinly sliced
6 oz bacon, chopped
16 cherry tomatoes, halved
(12 oz skinless cod or halibut
   fillet, cut into cubes
finely grated zest of 1 lemon
2 large handfuls of
   fresh spinach
1 cup crumbled feta cheese
crusty bread, to serve

Serves 4
Prep time 15 minutes
Cooking time 10 minutes

LEMONY SHRIMP & Broccoli Stir-Fry

3 tablespoons vegetable oil
1 large red onion, sliced
1 bunch of scallions, trimmed
  and coarsely chopped
3 cups small broccoli florets
8 oz cooked peeled shrimp
finely grated zest and juice of
  1 lemon
3 tablespoons light soy sauce
1 (6 oz) package ready-to-eat
  rice or noodles
salt

Serves **4**
Prep time **10 minutes**
Cooking time **15 minutes**

1 Heat the oil in a skillet, add the onion, and sauté over medium-high heat for about 5 minutes, stirring frequently, until softened. Add the scallions, broccoli, and shrimp and stir-fry for 4 minutes.

2 Add the lemon zest and juice and soy sauce to the pan and stir well, then add the rice and stir-fry until all the ingredients are piping hot and well mixed. Serve immediately.

Piri Piri Shrimp
& B E A N S

1 Put the garlic and chiles onto a square of heavy-duty aluminum foil. Bring the foil up and seal loosely, then tuck between hot coals or logs to cook for about 30 minutes, until softened.

2 Mix together the shrimp, beans, piquillo peppers, oil, vinegar, and parsley in a bowl, then spoon the mixture into the centers of four large squares of heavy-duty foil.

3 Carefully remove the garlic and chiles from the first foil package. Squeeze the garlic from their skins and add a clove and a chile half to each shrimp portion. Season with salt, then bring the foil up around the filling and seal well.

4 Tuck the packages between hot coals or logs to cook for 20-40 minutes, or until the shrimp turn pink and are cooked through. Rotate the packages during cooking.

5 Toast the bread on a grill rack over the barbecue grill or campfire until lightly charred.

6 Carefully open up the packages, spread the garlic over the toast, and pile the shrimp and beans on top.

4 garlic cloves, unpeeled
2 red or green chiles, seeded and halved
10 oz raw peeled shrimp
1 (15 oz) can navy beans, drained
¾ cup drained and diced piquillo peppers from a jar
⅓ cup olive oil
2 tablespoons sherry vinegar or white wine vinegar
3 tablespoons chopped parsley
salt
baguette or ciabatta slices, to serve

Serves 4
Prep time **20 minutes**
Cooking time **¾-1¼ hours**

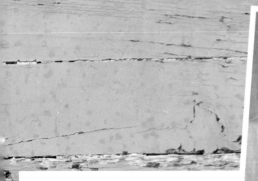

TUNA & OLIVE PASTA

1 Heat the oil in a large saucepan, add the onion, and sauté over medium heat for about 5 minutes, until softened. Add the garlic and sauté for another 1 minute.

2 Add the diced tomatoes and dried red pepper flakes, if using, and bring to a simmer, then cook gently for about 10 minutes, until thickened slightly.

3 Stir the tuna and olives into the sauce, add the pasta, and toss together. Heat through until piping hot.

3 tablespoons olive oil
1 red onion, sliced
2 garlic cloves, chopped
2 (14½ oz) cans diced tomatoes
½ teaspoon dried red pepper flakes (optional)
1 (5 oz) can chunk light tuna in water or oil, drained and flaked
¾ cup coarsely chopped pitted black or green olives
cooked penne or other pasta (see page 10), to serve

Serves **4**
Prep time **10 minutes**
Cooking time **20 minutes**

Tuna Fish Cakes

2 (12 oz) cans chunk light tuna
   in olive oil, drained
1¼ cups ricotta cheese
6 scallions, finely chopped
grated zest and juice of 1 lime
1 tablespoon chopped dill
1 egg, beaten
3 tablespoons olive oil
3½ cups leafy greens, such as
   arugula, mâche, or mizuna
salt and black pepper

Garlic and herb mayonnaise
1 crushed garlic clove,
   plus extra if required
2 teaspoons lime juice
1 tablespoon chopped
   fresh cilantro
pinch of cayenne pepper
¾ cup mayonnaise

Serves 4
Prep time **20 minutes**
Cooking time **20 minutes**

1 Flake the tuna into a bowl and beat in the ricotta, scallions, lime zest, dill, egg, and salt and black pepper to taste. Reserve 2 teaspoons of the lime juice and beat the remainder into the tuna mixture. Divide into 12 and shape into small cakes about 3 inches in diameter.

2 Heat 1 tablespoon of the oil in a skillet, add half the fish cakes, and cook over medium heat for 4-5 minutes on each side, until golden and heated through. (Cook for slightly longer over low heat if they start to overbrown.) Transfer to a plate, cover with aluminum foil, and keep warm. Repeat with another tablespoon of oil and the remaining fish cakes.

3 Meanwhile, to make the garlic mayonnaise, mix together the garlic, lime juice, cilantro, cayenne, and mayonnaise in a bowl. Taste and add more garlic, if desired.

4 Whisk together the remaining oil and lime juice in a bowl and toss with the leafy greens. Serve the fish cakes with the arugula salad and mayonnaise.

CREAMY SCALLOPS
WITH LEEKS

1 Melt half the butter in a skillet and cook the scallops and
bacon over high heat for 2 minutes, stirring frequently, until
just golden and cooked through. Transfer to a plate, cover with
aluminum foil, and keep warm.

2 Add the remaining butter to the pan and cook the
leeks over medium heat for about 5 minutes, stirring
occasionally, until softened and lightly browned in places. Add
the crème fraîche or sour cream and lemon zest and season
well with black pepper.

3 Return the scallops to the pan and toss into the creamy
leeks. Serve immediately with crusty bread.

4 tablespoons butter
16 shelled and cleaned scallops,
 halved
1 bacon slice, coarsely snipped
3 leeks, trimmed and sliced
1 cup crème fraîche or
 sour cream
finely grated zest of 1 lemon
black pepper
crusty bread, to serve

Serves 4
Prep time **10 minutes**
Cooking time **10 minutes**

CAMPING TIP

For scallop kebabs for the barbecue,
cut 8 bacon slices in half and
wrap around each scallop. Thread
4 scallops each onto 4 metal kebab
skewers and brush with olive oil.
Cook for 2–3 minutes on each
side until brown.

CAMPFIRE
FISH STEW WITH BASIL & MOZZARELLA TOASTS

1 Heat half the oil in a large saucepan and sauté the shallots until softened. Add the squid and cook until opaque. Transfer to a plate and cover with aluminum foil.

2 Add the remaining oil to the pan with the bell peppers and sauté for 10-15 minutes, until softened. Stir in the garlic, tomato puree or sauce, capers, sugar, and stock or broth. Crumble in the saffron and bring to a simmer. Cover with a lid and cook for about 45 minutes, or until the bell peppers are tender.

3 Meanwhile, to make the toasts, split the pitas along one edge and spread one side of each cavity with the pesto. Top with the mozzarella slices, basil leaves, and a little salt and black pepper.

4 Cut the fish into large chunks, discarding any stray bones. Stir into the stew with the squid and shallots and cook for about 5 minutes, or until the fish is cooked through.

5 While the fish is cooking, put the toasts on the grill rack and cook until lightly browned. Alternatively, wrap them individually in aluminum foil and tuck between hot coals or logs to heat.

6 Season the stew with salt and black pepper and serve with the toasts.

⅓ cup olive oil
6 shallots, finely sliced
8 squid tubes, cut into rings
2 red bell peppers, cored, seeded, and cut into small chunks
4 garlic cloves, finely chopped
¾ cup tomato puree or tomato sauce
2 tablespoons capers, drained
1 teaspoon sugar
2 cups hot fish or chicken stock or broth
½ teaspoon saffron strands
2 lb mixed white fish fillets, such as Alaskan pollock, cod, halibut, monkfish, red snapper, or sea bass, skinned
salt and black pepper

Basil and mozzarella toasts
4 pita breads
2 tablespoons pesto
4 oz mozzarella, thinly sliced
handful of basil leaves, shredded

Serves 4
Prep time **30 minutes**
Cooking time **about 1¼ hours**

Paella

1 Heat half the oil in a paella pan or large skillet, add the shrimp, and cook until they turn pink and are cooked through. Transfer to a plate. Add the chicken to the pan and cook until golden.

2 Add the remaining oil to the pan with the chorizo, bell pepper, and onion and sauté until the onion is soft and the chorizo has turned the oil golden. Add the rice and stir to combine, then crumble the saffron over the top.

3 Pour in the stock or broth and bring to a gentle simmer. Place the pan over an area of the fire that's not too hot and cover with a lid or aluminum foil. Cook gently for 20-30 minutes, or until the rice is tender and the chicken is cooked through. Drizzle a little hot water over the rice to stop it from drying out, if necessary.

4 Return the shrimp to the pan and sprinkle with the mussels, if using. Replace the cover to trap in the steam and cook for another few minutes until the mussels have opened up. Discard any mussels that remain closed. Season with salt and black pepper and serve with lemon wedges.

½ cup olive oil
8 large raw peeled shrimp
4 boneless, skinless chicken thighs, cut into small chunks
4 oz chorizo sausage, diced
1 red or green bell pepper, cored, seeded, and diced
1 onion, chopped
1¼ cups paella or risotto rice
large pinch of saffron strands
2 cups hot chicken or fish stock or broth
8 oz fresh mussels, scrubbed and debearded (optional)
salt and black pepper
lemon wedges, to serve

Serves 4
Prep time **20 minutes**
Cooking time **40-50 minutes**

SPINACH, RICOTTA, & Basil Penne

1 tablespoon olive oil
1 teaspoon chopped garlic
3 cups finely chopped
   fresh spinach
2 tablespoons chopped basil
1 cup ricotta cheese
½ cup dry white wine
salt and black pepper

To serve
cooked penne or other pasta
   (see page 10)
Parmesan cheese shavings

Serves **4**
Prep time **5 minutes**
Cooking time **6-8 minutes**

1 Heat the oil in a large saucepan, add the garlic, and cook for 2 minutes. Stir in the spinach and cook for 1-2 minutes, until wilted. Add the basil, ricotta, and wine, season with salt and black pepper, and cook gently until the ricotta has melted.

2 Stir the pasta into the ricotta mixture, toss well, and heat through until piping hot. Serve topped with Parmesan shavings and freshly ground black pepper.

TOMATO, ROSEMARY, & CANNELLINI BEAN STEW

1 Heat the oil in a skillet, add the onion, and sauté over medium heat for about 5 minutes, stirring occasionally, until softened. Add the garlic paste and rosemary and cook, stirring constantly, for another 30 seconds.

2 Add the beans and tomato sauce and bring to a boil. Cover with a lid and simmer gently for about 7 minutes, or until piping hot. Serve with crusty bread for mopping up the juices.

3 tablespoons olive oil
1 large red onion, sliced
2 teaspoons garlic paste
2 tablespoons chopped
  rosemary leaves
2 (15 oz) cans cannellini beans,
  drained
2 cups prepared tomato sauce
crusty bread, to serve

Serves **4**
Prep time **5 minutes**
Cooking time **15 minutes**

LENTIL *Stew*

1 Heat the oil in a large saucepan, add the bell peppers, onion, garlic, and fennel, and cook over medium-high heat for about 5 minutes, stirring frequently, until softened and lightly browned.

2 Stir in the lentils, stock or broth, and wine and bring to a boil, then cover with a lid and simmer gently for about 25 minutes or until the lentils are tender.

3 Serve the stew hot, with garlic bread for mopping up the juices.

¼ cup olive oil
1 red bell pepper, cored, seeded, and cut into chunks
1 green bell pepper, cored, seeded, and cut into chunks
1 red onion, coarsely chopped
1 garlic clove, sliced
1 fennel bulb, trimmed and sliced
1¼ cups dried green lentils, rinsed
2½ cups hot vegetable stock or broth
1¼ cups red wine
Garlic Bread (see page 206), to serve

Serves **4**
Prep time **10 minutes**
Cooking time **35 minutes**

Speedy
KIDNEY BEAN & CILANTRO
Curry

2 teaspoons vegetable oil
1 teaspoon cumin seeds
1 tablespoon tomato paste
2 teaspoons curry powder
1 teaspoon ground turmeric
1 teaspoon ground coriander
1 teaspoon ground cumin
2 teaspoons garam masala
1 (15 oz) can kidney beans, drained
2 scallions, sliced
2 tablespoons chopped fresh cilantro
salt
mixed leafy greens, such as arugula, mâche, or mizuna, and warm pita breads, to serve

1 Heat the oil in a skillet, add the cumin seeds, and let them pop for a few seconds. Stir in the tomato paste, curry powder, ground spices, and garam masala and blend well together over low heat.

2 Mix in the kidney beans, scallions, and chopped cilantro and heat through. Add salt to taste and stir in a few tablespoons of hot water, if you prefer more sauce. Serve the curry hot with mixed leafy greens or in warm pita breads.

Serves 4
Prep time **5 minutes**
Cooking time **10 minutes**

SICILIAN SPAGHETTI

2 (2 oz) cans anchovy fillets
in olive oil
2 teaspoons chopped garlic
⅓ cup chopped flat leaf parsley
¼ teaspoon dried red
pepper flakes (optional)
juice of 3 lemons
½ cup grated Parmesan cheese
black pepper

To serve
cooked spaghetti (see page 10)
arugula salad

Serves 4
Prep time **5 minutes**
Cooking time **10 minutes**

1 Drain the olive oil from the anchovies into a skillet and add the garlic. Cook over medium heat for 1 minute, then add the anchovies and cook for 2-3 minutes, until the anchovies begin to soften and break up. Add the parsley and dried red pepper flakes, if using, then stir in the lemon juice.

2 Add the pasta, season with black pepper, toss well, and heat through until piping hot. Stir in most of the Parmesan, reserving a little for garnish.

3 Sprinkle the pasta with the reserved Parmesan and serve with an arugula salad.

Basil & Tomato Stew

1 Quarter and seed the tomatoes, scooping out the pulp into a strainer over a bowl to catch the juices.

2 Heat ¼ cup of the oil in a large saucepan, add the onions and celery, and cook over medium heat for about 5 minutes, until softened. Add the garlic and mushrooms and cook for another 3 minutes.

3 Add the tomatoes and their juices, tomato paste, stock or broth, sugar, and capers and bring to a boil, then simmer gently for about 5 minutes.

4 Tear the herbs into pieces, add to the pan with a little salt and black pepper, and cook for 1 minute. Ladle into bowls, drizzle with the remaining oil, and serve with crusty bread.

8 ripe tomatoes (about 2 lb), skinned
⅓ cup olive oil
2 onions, chopped
4 celery sticks, sliced
4 plump garlic cloves, thinly sliced
3 cups sliced white mushrooms
3 tablespoons tomato paste
2½ cups vegetable stock or broth
1 tablespoon packed light brown sugar
3 tablespoons drained capers
large handful of basil leaves
large handful of chervil or flat leaf parsley
salt and black pepper
crusty bread, to serve

Serves 4
Prep time 15 minutes
Cooking time 15 minutes

CAMPING TIP

Invest in a head flashlight—it will be the most indispensable piece of equipment on your camping trip (apart from the tent possibly). From after-dark dinner prep to nocturnal calls of nature, the head flashlight is essential for hands-free activities.

RATATOUILLE

¼ cup olive oil
2 large onions, thinly sliced
3 large garlic cloves, crushed
2 large red bell peppers, cored, seeded, and cut into squares
1 large yellow bell pepper, cored, seeded, and cut into squares
2 extra-large eggplants, quartered lengthwise and cut into ½ inch cubes
2 zucchini, cut into ½ inch cubes
2 tablespoons tomato paste
1 (14½ oz) can plum or roma tomatoes
12 basil leaves, chopped
1 tablespoon finely chopped marjoram or oregano
1 teaspoon finely chopped thyme
1 tablespoon paprika
2-4 tablespoons finely chopped parsley
salt and black pepper
crusty bread, to serve

1   Heat the oil in a large saucepan, add the onions and garlic, and cook over medium heat for 5-10 minutes, until softened but not browned. Add the bell peppers and cook for another 5 minutes, then stir in the eggplants and zucchini.

2   Add the tomato paste, plum or roma tomatoes, basil, majoram or oregano, thyme, and paprika and season with salt and black pepper.

3   Stir to combine and bring to a boil, then cover with a lid and simmer gently for 20-30 minutes, or until the vegetables are tender and the sauce is thickened.

4   Stir in the parsley and adjust the seasoning, if necessary. Serve hot or cold with crusty bread.

Serves **8**
Prep time **15 minutes**
Cooking time **35-50 minutes**

Fava Bean, Lemon, & PARMESAN RISOTTO

1 Heat the butter and oil in a large saucepan. Add the onion and garlic and sauté gently for about 5 minutes, until softened. Add the rice and cook for another 1 minute, stirring.

2 Add the wine and cook, stirring regularly, until the wine is absorbed. Add a little stock or broth and cook, stirring, until almost absorbed. Continue in the same way, gradually adding more stock or broth, until half of it has been used. Stir in the beans.

3 Gradually add the remaining stock or broth until the mixture is thickened and creamy but still retaining a little bite. This will take 15-20 minutes.

4 Stir in the Parmesan and lemon zest and juice, then season with salt and black pepper. Serve with extra Parmesan cheese.

2 tablespoons butter
2 tablespoons olive oil
1 onion, chopped
2 garlic cloves, crushed
2 cups risotto rice
²/₃ cup dry white wine
5 cups hot vegetable stock or broth
1 cup fresh fava beans
½ cup grated Parmesan cheese, plus extra to serve
zest and juice of 1 lemon
salt and black pepper

Serves 4
Prep time **5 minutes**
Cooking time **20-25 minutes**

Mushroom STROGANOFF

1 tablespoon vegetable oil
1 large onion, thinly sliced
4 celery sticks, thinly sliced
2 garlic cloves, crushed
1¼ lb mushrooms, chopped
2 teaspoons smoked paprika
1 cup hot vegetable stock or broth
²/₃ cup sour cream
black pepper

Serves 4
Prep time **10 minutes**
Cooking time **25 minutes**

1 Heat the oil in a skillet, add the onion, celery, and garlic, and sauté for about 5 minutes, until beginning to soften. Add the mushrooms and paprika and cook for another 5 minutes.

2 Pour in the stock or broth and cook for another 10 minutes, or until the liquid is reduced by half.

3 Stir in the sour cream and season with black pepper to taste. Cook over medium heat for 5 minutes. Serve immediately.

COCONUT DHAL
with Toasted Naan Strips

1 tablespoon vegetable oil
1 onion, coarsely chopped
2 tablespoons curry paste
²/₃ cup split red lentils, rinsed
1¾ cups coconut milk
naans or other flat breads,
   to serve

Serves 4
Prep time 5 minutes
Cooking time 20 minutes

1 Heat the oil in a saucepan, add the onion, and sauté over high heat, stirring, for 1 minute, then stir in the curry paste and lentils.

2 Pour in the coconut milk, then add 1¾ cups of water to the lentils. Bring to a boil, then simmer briskly, uncovered, for about 10 minutes, or until the lentils are tender and the mixture is thick and pulpy.

3 Meanwhile, lightly toast the naans or other flat bread on a grill rack over a barbecue grill or campfire until warm and golden. Cut into strips and serve alongside the dhal for dipping.

PANEER, PEA, & SPINACH *Curry*

2 tablespoons vegetable oil
1 onion, chopped
1 teaspoon chopped garlic
2 teaspoons peeled and
   chopped fresh ginger root
2 tablespoons medium curry
   powder
8 oz paneer cheese, cut into
   ¾ inch cubes
1¾ cups coconut milk
1⅔ cups fresh shelled peas
1 (6 oz) package fresh
   baby spinach
salt and black pepper
naans or other flat breads,
   to serve

1 Heat the oil in a large saucepan, add the onion, garlic, and ginger, and sauté over medium heat for about 5 minutes, until softened. Add the curry powder and cook for 1 minute, then stir in the paneer and stir-fry for another 1 minute.

2 Pour in the coconut milk, add the peas, and bring to a simmer. Cover with a lid and simmer for about 5 minutes, or until the peas are tender.

3 Stir in the spinach and cook for another 1 minute, until wilted. Season with salt and black pepper and serve with naans or other flat breads.

Serves **4**
Prep time **10 minutes**
Cooking time **15 minutes**

MIXED VEGETABLE
CURRY

1 Heat the oil in a large saucepan, add the onion, and cook over medium heat, stirring occasionally, for about 10 minutes, or until softened and golden. Alternatively, add the cumin seeds and cook, stirring frequently, until they sizzle.

2 Add the vegetables, chili powder, coriander, turmeric, and salt to taste and cook for 2-3 minutes, stirring constantly.

3 Stir in the tomatoes or lemon juice. If a dry vegetable curry is preferred, add only a little water, cover with a lid, and cook gently for 10-12 minutes, until dry. For a more moist curry, stir in 1¼ cups of water, cover, and simmer for 5-6 minutes, until the vegetables are tender. Serve with naans or other flat bread.

2-3 tablespoons vegetable oil
1 small onion, chopped, or
   2 teaspoons cumin seeds
1 (1 lb) package mixed
   vegetables (such as potatoes,
   carrots, and cauliflower, cut
   into chunks or broken into
   florets, green beans left
   whole, and peas)
about 1 teaspoon chili powder
2 teaspoons ground coriander
½ teaspoon ground turmeric
2-3 tomatoes, chopped, or juice
   of 1 lemon
salt
naans or other flat breads,
   to serve

Serves **4**
Prep time **15 minutes**
Cooking time **20-30 minutes**

3 tablespoons olive oil
1 onion, finely chopped
2 celery sticks, thinly sliced
2 garlic cloves, thinly sliced
2 (15 oz) cans lima beans,
  drained
1/4 cup tomato paste
3 3/4 cups hot vegetable stock
  or broth
1 tablespoon chopped rosemary
  or thyme
salt and black pepper
Parmesan cheese shavings,
  to serve

Serves **4**
Prep time **5 minutes**
Cooking time **20-25 minutes**

LIMA BEAN, ONION, & TOMATO SOUP

ALTHOUGH IT TAKES ONLY A FEW MINUTES TO
PREPARE, THIS CHUNKY SOUP DISTINCTLY RESEMBLES
A ROBUST ITALIAN MINESTRONE. IT MAKES A WORTHY
MAIN DISH SERVED WITH PLENTY OF BREAD.

1 Heat the oil in a saucepan, add the onion, and sauté for about 3 minutes, until beginning to soften. Add the celery and garlic and sauté for another 2 minutes.

2 Add the lima beans, tomato paste, stock or broth, rosemary or thyme, and a little salt and black pepper. Bring to a boil, then cover with a lid and simmer gently for 15 minutes. Serve sprinkled with the Parmesan shavings.

BLACK BEAN
& CABBAGE STEW

¼ cup olive oil
1 large onion, chopped
1 leek, trimmed and chopped
3 garlic cloves, sliced
1 tablespoon paprika
2 tablespoons chopped
   marjoram or thyme
5 red-skinned or white round
   potatoes (about 1¼ lb), cut
   into small chunks
1 (15 oz) can black beans or
   black-eyed peas, drained
4¼ cups hot vegetable stock
   or broth
2 cups shredded cabbage or
   collard greens
salt and black pepper
chunky bread, to serve

Serves **4**
Prep time **10 minutes**
Cooking time **25 minutes**

1 Heat the oil in a large saucepan, add the onion and leek, and sauté over medium heat for 3 minutes. Add the garlic and paprika and cook for another 2 minutes, until the vegetables are softened.

2 Add the marjoram or thyme, potatoes, beans, and stock or broth and bring to a boil. Cover with a lid and simmer gently for about 10 minutes, or until the potatoes have softened but are not mushy.

3 Add the cabbage or collard greens and season with salt and black pepper. Simmer for another 5 minutes. Serve the stew with chunky bread.

HEARTY DHAL, BUTTERNUT,
& SPINACH STEW

2 tablespoons vegetable oil
1 large onion, chopped
1 tablespoon medium curry
  paste
4¼ cups hot vegetable stock
  or broth
1 cup dried yellow split peas,
  rinsed
½ butternut squash, seeded,
  peeled, and cut into ¾ inch
  chunks
8 cups fresh baby spinach
salt
warm naans or flat breads,
  to serve

Serves **4**
Prep time **10 minutes**
Cooking time **about**
50 minutes

1 Heat the oil in a large saucepan, add the onion, and sauté, stirring, for about 5 minutes, until softened. Add the curry paste, stock or broth, and split peas and bring to a simmer. Cover with a lid and cook gently for 20 minutes, or until the split peas have softened.

2 Stir in the squash and cook for another 20 minutes, or until the split peas and squash are tender. Add the spinach, stirring it in until wilted, adding a little hot water if the stew has dried out. Season with a little salt and serve with warm bread.

CANNELLINI BEANS ON TOAST

2 tablespoons vegetable oil
1 onion, chopped
1 celery stick, thinly sliced
1 teaspoon cornstarch
1 (15 oz) can cannellini beans,
  drained
1 cup canned diced tomatoes
1¼ cups hot vegetable stock
1 tablespoon coarse-grain
  mustard
1 tablespoon molasses
1 tablespoon ketchup
1 tablespoon Worcestershire
  sauce
slices of chunky bread
salt and black pepper

Serves 2-3
Prep time **5 minutes**
Cooking time **25-30 minutes**

1 Heat the oil in a saucepan, add the onion and celery, and sauté for about 5 minutes, until golden and softened. Blend the cornstarch with 2 tablespoons water and add to the pan with the remaining ingredients.

2 Bring to a boil, then simmer, uncovered, for about 20 minutes, stirring frequently, until the mixture is thickened and pulpy.

3 Toast the bread on a grill rack over a barbecue grill or campfire until lightly charred. Serve the beans on the toast.

COOKING TIP

To add an extra spicy kick to your beans, add a dash of hot pepper sauce to the saucepan 5 minutes before the end of cooking time.

SPANISH TORTILLA

1 Heat 1 tablespoon of the olive oil in a skillet, add the onions and garlic, and sauté over medium heat for about 5 minutes, until golden and softened, then add the cooked potatoes and heat through.

2 Meanwhile, in a large bowl, beat together the eggs and milk. Add the potatoes, onion, and garlic to the egg mixture and stir well.

3 Return the pan to the heat and heat the remaining oil. Pour the potato-and-egg mixture into the pan and cook over low heat for 7–8 minutes, or until beginning to set. Place an inverted plate over the pan and turn the pan and plate together to transfer the tortilla onto the plate. Slide back into the pan and cook until golden and set underneath.

4 Turn out the tortilla onto a plate and let cool. Cut into slices and serve warm or cold.

2 tablespoons olive oil
2 onions, sliced
1 garlic clove, crushed
1 lb new potatoes, cooked
   and sliced (about 3 cups)
6 eggs
¼ cup milk

Serves **8**
Prep time **10 minutes**
Cooking time **20-25 minutes**

VEGETABLE & TOFU
STIR-FRY

3 tablespoons vegetable oil
10 oz firm tofu, cubed
1 onion, sliced
2 carrots, sliced
¼ head of broccoli, broken into
   small florets and stems sliced
1 red bell pepper, cored, seeded,
   and sliced
1 large zucchini, sliced
2 cups sugar snap peas
2 tablespoons soy sauce
2 tablespoons sweet chili sauce

To serve
chopped red chiles
Thai or ordinary basil leaves

Serves **4**
Prep time **10 minutes**
Cooking time **7 minutes**

1 Heat 1 tablespoon of the oil in a skillet until starting to smoke, add the tofu, and stir-fry over high heat for 2 minutes, until golden. Transfer to a plate with a slotted spoon.

2 Heat the remaining oil in the pan, add the onion and carrots, and stir-fry for 1½ minutes. Add the broccoli and red bell pepper and stir-fry for 1 minute, then add the zucchini and sugar snap peas and stir-fry for 1 minute.

3 Combine the soy and chili sauces and ½ cup of water, then add to the pan with the tofu. Cook for 1 minute. Serve sprinkled with chopped red chiles and basil leaves.

Stir-Fried VEGETABLE NOODLES

1 Heat the oil in a skillet, add the scallions and carrots, and stir-fry for 3 minutes. Add the garlic, dried red pepper flakes, snow peas, and mushrooms and stir-fry for 2 minutes. Add the napa cabbage and stir-fry for 1 minute.

2 Add the noodles to the pan with the soy sauce and hoisin sauce. Stir-fry over gentle heat for about 3–4 minutes, or until heated through. Serve immediately.

¼ cup vegetable oil
1 bunch of scallions, sliced
2 carrots, thinly sliced
2 garlic cloves, crushed
¼ teaspoon dried red pepper flakes
2 cups snow peas
4 oz shiitake mushrooms, halved
3 napa cabbage leaves, shredded
8 oz fresh medium egg noodles
2 tablespoons light soy sauce
3 tablespoons hoisin sauce

Serves **4**
Prep time **10 minutes**
Cooking time **10 minutes**

**LINGUINE WITH SHREDDED
HAM & EGGS**

JAMAICAN SALMON

TUNA QUESADILLA

CORN FRITTERS

QUICK & EASY

CRISPY LAMB MOROCCAN ROLLS

8 oz ground lamb
1 teaspoon ground cinnamon
3 tablespoons pine nuts
2 naans or other flat breads, warmed
¾ cup hummus
2 tablespoons mint leaves
1 small butterhead lettuce, finely shredded (optional)

Serves **2**
Prep time **15 minutes**
Cooking time **about 10 minutes**

1 Heat a skillet until hot, add the ground lamb, and cook for about 10 minutes, until golden brown, breaking it up with a wooden spoon. Add the cinnamon and pine nuts and cook for another 1 minute. Remove the lamb from the heat.

2 Place the warm naans or flat breads on a board and, using a rolling pin, firmly roll to flatten.

3 Mix the hummus with half the mint leaves, then spread in a thick layer over the naans or flat breads. Spoon the mixture over the crispy lamb, then sprinkle with the shredded lettuce, if using, and the remaining mint leaves. Roll up tightly, cut in half, and serve, wrapped in aluminum foil, if desired.

Linguine
WITH SHREDDED HAM & EGGS

THIS RECIPE IS PUT TOGETHER IN MINUTES AND IS CONVENIENTLY ADAPTABLE. USE OTHER SHREDDED, COOKED MEATS INSTEAD OF THE HAM IF YOU PREFER

3 tablespoons chopped
  flat leaf parsley
1 tablespoon coarse-grain
  mustard
2 teaspoons lemon juice
good pinch of sugar
3 tablespoons olive oil
4 oz thinly sliced ham
2 scallions
2 eggs
4 oz dried linguine
salt and black pepper

Serves **2**
Prep time **10 minutes**
Cooking time **10 minutes**

1 Mix together the parsley, mustard, lemon juice, sugar, oil, and a little salt and black pepper in a bowl and set aside. Roll up the ham and slice it as thinly as possible. Trim the scallions, cut them lengthwise into thin shreds, then cut into 2 inch lengths.

2 Put the eggs into a small saucepan and just cover with cold water. Bring to a boil and cook for 4 minutes (once the water boils the eggs will usually start to move around).

3 Meanwhile, cook the pasta in a saucepan of salted water for 6-8 minutes, or according to the package directions, until just tender. Add the scallions and cook for another 30 seconds.

4 Drain the pasta and return to the pan. Stir in the ham and the mustard dressing and pile onto plates. Shell and halve the eggs and serve on top.

Meatballs,
PEAS, & PASTA

1 Cut the sausage meat into small pieces and roll into walnut-size meatballs. Heat half the oil in a skillet, add the meatballs, and cook over medium heat, stirring frequently, for about 10 minutes, or until cooked through. Transfer to a plate, cover with aluminum foil, and keep warm.

2 Meanwhile, cook the pasta in a large saucepan of lightly salted boiling water for 8-10 minutes or according to the package directions. Add the peas to the last 4 minutes of the cooking time, return to a boil, and cook for another 4 minutes, or until the peas and pasta are just tender. Drain well, reserving ¼ cup of the cooking water, then return to the pan.

3 Add the garlic, sage, dried red pepper flakes, and salt and black pepper to taste to the meatball pan and cook over low heat for 2-3 minutes, until the garlic is soft but not browned. Stir in the meatballs.

4 Add the meatball mixture, reserved cooking water, and remaining oil to the pasta pan and heat through. Serve topped with grated Parmesan.

1 lb beef or pork link sausages, skins removed
¼ cup olive oil
12 oz dried fusilli
1⅔ cups shelled fresh peas
2 garlic cloves, sliced
2 tablespoons chopped sage
½ teaspoon dried red pepper flakes
salt and black pepper
grated Parmesan cheese, to serve

Serves **4**
Prep time **20 minutes**
Cooking time **15 minutes**

Pappardelle WITH
FIGS, GORGONZOLA, & PROSCIUTTO

THIS RECIPE COMBINES SWEET AND SALTY FLAVORS, TOSSED IN A HONEY AND ORANGE DRESSING AND MAKES A GREAT LIGHT LUNCH.

1 Cook the pasta in a large saucepan of salted boiling water for 2-3 minutes for fresh and 8-10 minutes for dried or according to the package directions.

2 Meanwhile, whisk together the honey, mustard, orange and lemon juices, oil, and a little salt and black pepper in a bowl.

3 Drain the pasta and return it to the saucepan. Gently mix in the figs, prosciutto, and Gorgonzola. Serve with the dressing spooned over the top.

8 oz fresh or dried pappardelle
2 tablespoons honey
2 teaspoons coarse-grain mustard
3 tablespoons orange juice
squeeze of lemon juice
3 tablespoons olive oil
4 ripe, juicy figs, cut into thin wedges
4 oz prosciutto, torn into small pieces
5 oz Gorgonzola cheese, coarsely diced
salt and black pepper

Serves 4
Prep time **10 minutes**
Cooking time **2-10 minutes**

GRILLED TURKEY
& Cheese Rolls

4 flat rolls
2 tablespoons whole-grain
   mustard
2 tablespoons cranberry sauce
8 oz cooked turkey breast,
   sliced
1 cup shredded Swiss, cheddar,
   or American cheese

Serves 4
Prep time **5 minutes**
Cooking time **16 minutes**

1 Halve the rolls and spread half with the mustard and the other half with the cranberry sauce. Top with the turkey slices and cheese and sandwich together.

2 Heat a dry skillet until hot, add 2 sandwiches, and cook over medium-high heat for 4 minutes on each side, until golden and the cheese has melted. Serve hot.

3 Repeat with the remaining 2 sandwiches.

JAMAICAN SPICED
Salmon with Corn & Okra

4 skinless salmon fillets
(about 6 oz each)
1 tablespoon Jamaican jerk
seasoning
4 ears of corn, shucked
and halved
3 tablespoons olive oil
1 red onion, sliced
20 okra pods (about 8 oz),
trimmed
4 tablespoons butter
½ teaspoon paprika
½ teaspoon ground nutmeg
salt

Serves 4
Prep time **10 minutes**
Cooking time **15 minutes**

1 Rub each of the salmon fillets with the Jamaican jerk seasoning and set aside.

2 Cook the corn in a large saucepan of boiling water and cook for about 5 minutes, or until tender. Drain well.

3 Heat 2 tablespoons of the oil in a large saucepan, add the onion, and sauté over medium heat, stirring frequently, for 2 minutes. Add the okra and cook, stirring frequently, for about 4 minutes, until beginning to soften. Add the corn on the cobs to the pan with the butter and spices and toss for 2-3 minutes, until lightly browned in places.

4 Meanwhile, heat the remaining tablespoon of oil in a skillet and cook the salmon fillets, spice side down, over medium heat for 3-4 minutes, then turn over and cook for another 2 minutes, or until cooked through. Serve hot with the corn-and-okra mixture.

TUNA QUESADILLA
with Salsa

2 soft flour tortillas
¼ cup tomato salsa
2 scallions, coarsely chopped
1 (5 oz) can chunk light tuna in
  water, drained
⅓ cup drained canned corn
  kernels with red peppers
¾ cup shredded mozzarella
  cheese
olive oil, for brushing

Serves **2**
Prep time **5 minutes**
Cooking time **4-6 minutes**

1 Place 1 tortilla on a plate and spread with the salsa. Sprinkle with the scallions, tuna, corn, and cheese. Place the second tortilla on top and press down.

2 Heat a skillet and brush with oil. Place the quesadilla in the pan and cook over medium heat for 2-3 minutes, pressing down with a spatula until the cheese starts to melt.

3 Place an inverted plate over the pan and turn the pan and plate together to transfer the quesadilla to the plate. Slide back into the pan and cook for 2-3 minutes on the other side. Serve cut into wedges.

Pesto & SALMON PASTA

1 Cook the pasta in a large saucepan of lightly salted boiling water for about 8 minutes or according to the package directions, until almost tender.

2 Meanwhile, heat the oil in a skillet, add the onion, and sauté over medium heat for about 5 minutes, until softened.

3 Drain the salmon and discard skin and bones. Flake the flesh.

4 Add the peas to the pasta and cook for another 5 minutes, until just tender. Drain the pasta and peas, retaining a few tablespoons of the cooking water, and return to the pan.

5 Stir in the pesto, lemon juice, Parmesan, onion, reserved water, and flaked salmon. Season lightly with salt and black pepper and toss gently. Serve with extra Parmesan and leafy greens.

12 oz dried penne
2 tablespoons olive oil
1 onion, thinly sliced
1 (15 oz) can salmon
1 cup shelled fresh peas
2 tablespoons pesto
1 tablespoon lemon juice
1/3 cup grated Parmesan cheese, plus extra to serve
salt and black pepper
leafy greens, such as arugula, mâche, or mizuna, to serve

Serves 4
Prep time 10 minutes
Cooking time 15 minutes

PASTA SALAD WITH CRAB,
LIME, & ARUGULA

IF YOU MAKE THIS BEFORE YOU GO CAMPING, CONTINUE TO THE END OF
STEP 2, THEN PACK THE PASTA IN AN AIRTIGHT CONTAINER OR SEALABLE
FREEZER BAG AND STORE IN A COOLER. ADD THE TOMATOES AND ARUGULA
JUST BEFORE YOU'RE READY TO EAT.

2 oz dried pasta, such as
  rigatoni
grated zest and juice of ½ a lime
2 tablespoons crème fraîche or
  Greek yogurt
½ (6½ oz) can crabmeat,
  drained
8 cherry tomatoes, halved
handful of arugula

Serves 1
Prep time **5 minutes,
plus cooling**
Cooking time **10 minutes**

1 Cook the pasta in a saucepan of boiling water for about
10 minutes or according to the package directions, until
tender, then drain and let cool.

2 Mix together the lime zest and juice, crème fraîche or
Greek yogurt, and crabmeat in a large bowl. Add the
pasta and mix again.

3 Add the tomatoes and arugula to the bowl, toss
everything together, and serve.

CAMPING TIP

Buy yourself a cheap groundsheet or
tarpaulin and fold it to the same size
as your tent. Peg your tent out over
the groundsheet; when you pack up,
the bottom of your tent will be clean
and mud-free. You can clean the
groundsheet more easily than
the tent.

SHRIMP, MANGO, & AVOCADO *Wrap*

1 Mix together the crème fraîche or Greek yogurt and ketchup. Add a few drops of Tabasco sauce to taste. Add the shrimp, mango, and avocado and toss the mixture together.

2 Divide the mixture among the tortillas, add some leafy greens, then roll up and serve.

2 tablespoons crème fraîche or Greek yogurt
2 teaspoons ketchup
few drops of Tabasco sauce
10 oz cooked peeled shrimp
1 mango, peeled, pitted, and thinly sliced
1 avocado, peeled, pitted, and sliced
3½ cups leafy greens, such as mâche, mizuna, or arugula
4 flour tortillas

Serves **4**
Prep time **10 minutes**

GRILLED *Greek-Style* SANDWICHES

¼ small red onion, thinly sliced
8 cherry tomatoes, quartered
4 pitted black ripe olives,
   chopped
2 inch piece of cucumber,
   seeded and cut into small
   pieces
1 teaspoon dried oregano
⅓ cup crumbled feta cheese
1 teaspoon lemon juice
2 seeded pita breads
¼ cup shredded cheddar or
   Jarlsberg cheese
olive oil, for brushing
black pepper

Serves **2**
Prep time **15 minutes**
Cooking time **4-6 minutes**

1 Mix together the onion, tomatoes, olives, cucumber, oregano, and feta in a small bowl. Add the lemon juice, season with black pepper, and mix gently.

2 Slice each pita bread in half horizontally. Divide the feta mixture between the bottom halves of the pita breads, then add the cheddar or Jarlsberg. Cover with the top halves of the pita breads.

3 Brush a ridged grill pan or skillet with oil and heat over medium heat. When hot, add the sandwiches, press down gently with a spatula, and cook for 2-3 minutes on each side, or until golden and the cheese has melted. Serve immediately.

MEDITERRANEAN
Goat Cheese
OMELETS

¼ cup olive oil
3 cups halved cherry tomatoes
a little chopped basil
12 eggs
2 tablespoons whole-grain
  mustard
4 tablespoons butter
4 oz soft goat cheese, diced
salt and black pepper

Serves **4**
Prep time **15 minutes**
Cooking time **20-25 minutes**

1 Heat the oil in a skillet, add the tomatoes, and cook for 2-3 minutes, until they have softened; if necessary, do this in 2 batches. Add the basil and season with salt and black pepper, then transfer to a bowl, cover with aluminum foil, and keep warm.

2 Beat the eggs with the mustard in a bowl and season with salt and black pepper. Melt one-quarter of the butter in a skillet, then swirl in one-quarter of the egg mixture. Fork over the omelet so that it cooks evenly.

3 As soon as it is set on the bottom (but still a little runny in the middle), dot over one-quarter of the goat cheese and cook for another 30 seconds. Carefully slide the omelet onto a plate, folding it in half as you do so, and serve with one-quarter of the tomatoes.

4 Repeat with the remaining mixture to make 3 more omelets, and serve with the remaining tomatoes.

Caramelized Onion
& CHEESE CRÊPES

1¼ cups whole wheat flour
pinch of salt
1 egg, lightly beaten
1¼ cups milk
1 tablespoon mustard
vegetable oil, for frying

Filling
3 tablespoons butter
3 onions, thinly sliced
2 teaspoons caster sugar
a few thyme sprigs
8 oz Emmental or Gruyère
   cheese, grated
salt and black pepper

Serves 4
Prep time **10 minutes**
Cooking time **20-30 minutes**

1 Put the flour and salt in a bowl and make a well in the center. Pour the egg and some of the milk into the well, then beat, gradually incorporating the flour to make a smooth paste. Beat in the remaining milk and the mustard. Set aside.

2 To make the filling, melt the butter in a saucepan, add the onions and sugar, and cook over low heat for about 10-15 minutes, or until they are softened, deep golden, and caramelized. Tear the thyme leaves off the stems and add them to the pan with salt and plenty of pepper. Remove from the heat and keep warm.

3 Heat a little oil in a skillet until it starts to smoke, then pour off the excess into a cup. Pour a quarter of the batter into the pan, tilting it until the bottom is coated with a thin layer. Cook for 1-2 minutes, or until golden underneath. Carefully flip the crêpe over and cook for another 30-45 seconds until it is golden on the other side.

4 Add a quarter of the onions and cheese to one half of the crêpe and heat briefly until the cheese begins to melt, then flip over and slide onto a plate. Serve immediately.

5 Repeat with the remaining batter and filling to make 3 more crêpes, adding a little more oil to the pan as required.

EGG & MANCHEGO TORTILLAS

1 Beat the eggs with a fork in a bowl, then stir in the onion, chile, and corn. Season well with salt and black pepper.

2 Melt the butter in a large saucepan until foaming, add the egg mixture and cook over medium heat, stirring constantly, until the eggs are softly scrambled. Immediately remove the pan from the heat and stir in the crumbled Manchego and coriander.

3 Spoon onto the warm tortillas, sprinkle with green chile slices, fresh cilantro, and chives and top with shavings of Manchego. Serve with sweet chili sauce.

10 eggs
1 onion, finely chopped
1 green chile, seeded and finely chopped
4 tablespoons canned corn
2 tablespoons butter
3 oz Manchego cheese, crumbled
1 tablespoon chopped fresh cilantro
8 flour tortillas, warmed
salt and black pepper

To serve
green chile slices
fresh cilantro leaves
snipped chives
Manchego shavings
4 tablespoons sweet chili sauce

Serves **4**
Prep time **15 minutes**
Cooking time **about 5 minutes**

RICE NOODLES WITH
Green Beans & Ginger

4 oz fine rice noodles
1 cup halved green bean
finely grated zest and juice
    of 2 limes
1 Thai chile, seeded and finely
    chopped
1 inch piece of fresh ginger root,
    peeled and finely chopped
2 teaspoons sugar
small handful of fresh cilantro,
    chopped
⅓ cup chopped dried pineapple

1 Put the noodles into a heatproof bowl, cover with plenty of boiling water, and let stand for 4 minutes, or prepare according to package directions, until soft.

2 Meanwhile, cook the beans in a saucepan of boiling water for about 3 minutes, or until tender. Drain.

3 Mix together the lime zest and juice, chile, ginger, sugar, and cilantro in a small bowl.

4 Drain the noodles and place in a large bowl. Add the cooked beans, pineapple, and dressing and toss together lightly before serving.

Serves **4**
Prep time **10 minutes**
Cooking time **5 minutes**

CAMPING TIP

A double-handle wok is a great addition to your camping kitchen—you can use it as a makeshift dish-washing bowl or to carry things about.

RICE NOODLE PANCAKES
with Stir-Fried Vegetables

1 Cook the noodles in a saucepan of lightly salted boiling water for about 3 minutes, or until tender. Drain well. Transfer to a bowl, then add the chile, ginger, cilantro, flour, and 2 teaspoons of oil and mix well. Set aside.

2 Thinly slice the broccoli stems and cut the florets into small pieces. Cook the stems in boiling water for 30 seconds, add the florets, and cook for another 30 seconds. Drain the broccoli well.

3 Heat the 2 tablespoons vegetable oil in a skillet over high heat, add the onion, and stir-fry for 2 minutes. Add the bell peppers and stir-fry for 3 minutes, or until just softened. Stir in the cooked broccoli, sugar snap peas, hoisin sauce, and lime juice and season with salt and black pepper. Transfer to a bowl, cover with aluminum foil, and keep warm.

4 Heat some oil in the skillet to a depth of ½ inch. Place 4 large separate spoonfuls of the noodles (half the mixture) in the oil. Fry for about 5 minutes, until crisp and lightly browned. Drain the pancakes on paper towels and keep warm. Repeat with the remaining noodle mixture.

5 Reheat the vegetables for 1 minute, if necessary, then pile onto the noodle pancakes and serve.

6 oz dried wide rice noodles
1 green chile, seeded and sliced
1 inch piece of fresh ginger root, peeled and grated
3 tablespoons chopped fresh cilantro
2 teaspoons all-purpose flour
2 teaspoons vegetable oil, plus extra for pan-frying

Stir-fried vegetables
¼ head of broccoli
2 tablespoons vegetable oil
1 small onion, sliced
1 red bell pepper, cored, seeded, and sliced
1 yellow or orange bell pepper, cored, seeded, and sliced
2 cups halved sugar snap peas (halved lengthwise)
⅓ cup hoisin sauce
1 tablespoon lime juice
salt and black pepper

Serves 4
Prep time **15 minutes**
Cooking time **20 minutes**

CORN FRITTERS WITH SWEET CHILI DIP

2 cups all-purpose flour
2 eggs
½ cup milk
6 scallions, chopped
2 (11 oz) cans corn kernels,
  drained well
2 tablespoons vegetable oil,
  plus extra if required
salt and black pepper
fresh cilantro leaves, to garnish

Sweet chili dip
1 cup light cream cheese
2 tablespoons sweet chili sauce

Serves 4
Prep time **10 minutes**
Cooking time **20 minutes**

1 Put the flour into a bowl and make a well in the center. Break the eggs into the well and add the milk. Gradually whisk the flour into the eggs and milk to make a smooth, thick batter. Stir in the scallions and corn and season with salt and black pepper.

2 To make the dip, put the cream cheese into a bowl and stir to soften, then lightly stir through the sweet chili sauce to form a marbled effect.

3 Heat the oil in a skillet, add spoonfuls of the batter, about 4 at a time, and cook for 2 minutes on each side, or until golden, firm to the touch, and heated through. Serve the fritters warm with the dip, sprinkled with cilantro leaves.

4 Repeat with the remaining batter, adding extra oil, if necessary.

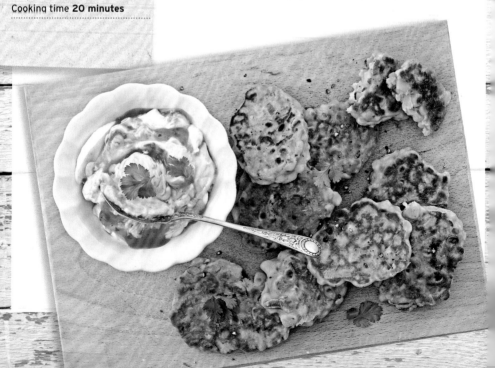

LEMON RICOTTA
& ZUCCHINI RIBBON
Stir-Fry

8 oz dried parpardelle or
  tagliatelle
4 small zucchini
salt and black pepper
green salad, to serve

Lemon ricotta
1 teaspoon fennel seeds
¼ teaspoon dried red pepper
  flakes (optional)
12-15 black peppercorns
1 cup ricotta cheese
¼ teaspoon ground nutmeg
finely grated zest and juice
  of 1 lemon

Serves **4**
Prep time **15 minutes**
Cooking time **about**
7 minutes

1 To make the lemony ricotta, lightly crush the fennel seeds with the dried red pepper flakes, if using, and black peppercorns, then put into a bowl. Add the ricotta, nutmeg, and lemon zest and juice and mix well, then set aside.

2 Cook the pasta in a saucepan of boiling water for about 8-10 minutes, or according to package directions, until just tender.

3 Meanwhile, slice the zucchini thinly into ribbons, using a sharp vegetable peeler.

4 Add the zucchini to the pasta 2 minutes before the end of the pasta cooking time, return to a boil, and cook for 2 minutes, or until the pasta is tender and the zucchini softened.

5 Drain the pasta and zucchini, reserving 2-3 tablespoons of the cooking liquid. Return the pasta, zucchini, and reserved water to the pan, add the ricotta, and stir gently to combine. Season with salt and black pepper, and serve with a green salad.

ENTERTAINMENT

Camping offers the ideal opportunity to enjoy some good, old-fashioned family entertainment. And let's face it: With everyone gathered together in a relatively small space—devoid of television and other modern media—you will need to get creative and plan activities to keep the kids amused during the day and to while away the evenings.

Daytime Activities

NATURE TRAIL

This can be as low-key or high-tech as you want. If you have the time, inclination, and knowledge of wildlife, you could prepare sheets of plants and animals to find. Or you can simply bundle the kids out of the tent and into the woods and see what you can find. Either way, you'll all get a good dose of fresh air and exercise and build up an appetite for dinner.

SPORTS DAY

Bring a jumping rope, basketball, tennis balls, Hula Hoops, or anything else that doesn't take up too much space in the car but can be easily adapted to set up an impromptu sports day on a sunny afternoon. Running races, wheelbarrow races, dribbling competitions, catching, balancing, jumping, and skipping can all be incorporated.

HIDE-AND-SEEK

No equipment is required for this game that will have the kids squealing in delight.

TREASURE HUNT

No explanation necessary!

Wet Weather Games

CARDS

Bring a couple of packs of cards. If you don't know many games, look some up online before you travel so you have something new for the family to play on rainy days.

PAPER AND PENS

From diaries to drawings, hangman to tic-tac-toe, a selection of note pads, pencils, and crayons are essential.

BOARD GAMES

It's always good to have a couple of favorite board games tucked away in the car in case the weather turns against you.

Around the Campfire

SCARY STORYTELLING

Before the trip, ask everyone to find a scary story that they can read out around the campfire. You can either designate an evening as "fright night" or pick someone different to tell their tale each night.

SONG TIME

A campfire isn't a campfire without some rusty guitar playing and drunken sing-alongs. If one of your party plays an instrument, it should be obligatory for them to bring it on the trip. If you're traveling with kids, involve them by asking them to choose songs or letting them put on a performance of their own.

CHARADES

This classic camping game will keep everyone entertained, especially after a couple of drinks.

CURRIED *Cauliflower,* LENTIL, & RICE

2 tablespoons vegetable oil
1 large onion, sliced
2 teaspoons cumin seeds
2 tablespoons curry paste
1 small head of cauliflower,
   cut into florets
½ cup red lentils, rinsed
¾ cup basmati or other
   long-grain rice
3 cups hot vegetable stock
   or broth
2 carrots, shredded
½ cup cashew nuts, toasted
2 handfuls of fresh cilantro
   leaves, to garnish

Serves 4
Prep time **10 minutes**
Cooking time **30 minutes**

1 Heat the oil in a skillet, add the onion, and sauté over medium heat for about 5 minutes, until softened. Add the cumin seeds and cook for 30 seconds, then add the curry paste and cook for another 30 seconds.

2 Add the cauliflower, red lentils, rice, and stock or broth and bring to a boil, then cover with a lid and simmer gently for 10-15 minutes, or until cooked through and the liquid is absorbed.

3 Stir in the carrots and cook for 2 minutes, adding a little hot water if the mixture is too dry. Sprinkle with the cashews and serve sprinkled with cilantro leaves.

BIG MAC 'N' CHEESE

8 oz macaroni
pinch of ground nutmeg
4 tablespoons butter
¼ cup all-purpose flour
2½ cups milk
2 teaspoons Dijon mustard
2 cups shredded cheddar or
   American cheese
4 small tomatoes,
   cut into wedges
salt and black pepper

Serves 4
Prep time **10 minutes**
Cooking time **20 minutes**

1 Cook the macaroni in a large saucepan of boiling water for 10-12 minutes, or according to package directions, until tender.

2 Drain the pasta. Dry the saucepan, then add the butter and heat until melted. Stir in the flour, then gradually add the milk and bring to a boil, stirring constantly, until thickened.

3 Stir in the mustard, cheese, and plenty of salt and black pepper and heat until the cheese has melted. Stir in the macaroni and tomatoes, and heat through.

CAMPING TIP

To keep your cooler as cold as possible if there are no refrigerators or freezers at the campsite, freeze whatever food you won't be eating on the first day and pack at the bottom of your cooler to defrost slowly and keep the box cold.

GREEN CHEESE PASTA

1 Cook the pasta shapes for 8-10 minutes in a saucepan of boiling water, or according to package directions, until just tender. Drain and set aside.

2 Meanwhile, rinse the spinach with water and coarsely drain, then cook in a hot skillet for about 2 minutes, until just wilted. Press out any water and chop finely, then return to the pan and toss with the nutmeg. Set aside.

3 Melt the butter in a saucepan. Remove from the heat, add the flour, and stir to form a thick paste. Return to the heat and cook gently for a few seconds, stirring constantly. Remove from the heat and gradually add the milk, stirring well after each addition. Return to the heat and bring to a boil, stirring constantly until the sauce has boiled and thickened.

4 Add the spinach, cheese, and pasta, stir well to coat, and heat through gently.

8 oz dried pasta shapes
1 (10 oz) package fresh spinach
1 teaspoon ground nutmeg
4 tablespoons butter
⅓ cup all-purpose flour
2½ cups milk
1 cup shredded cheddar cheese

Serves 4
Prep time 10 minutes
Cooking time 15-20 minutes

Refried Bean
QUESADILLA

¾ cup canned refried beans
2 scallions, chopped
⅓ cup drained canned
  corn kernels
1 tablespoon chopped fresh
  cilantro
2 soft corn tortillas
3 tablespoons tomato salsa,
  plus extra to serve
½ cup shredded cheddar or
  Monterey Jack cheese
olive oil, for brushing

Serves 2
Prep time **5 minutes**
Cooking time **4-6 minutes**

1 Mix together the refried beans, scallions, corn, and cilantro in a bowl.

2 Spread 1 tortilla with the bean mixture, top with the salsa, and sprinkle with the cheese. Cover the filling with the remaining tortilla.

3 Brush a skillet or ridged grill pan with oil and heat over medium heat. When hot, add the quesadilla and cook over medium heat for 2-3 minutes, pressing down with a spatula, until the cheese starts to melt.

4 Place a large plate over the pan and invert the quesadilla onto the plate. Return to the pan and cook for 2-3 minutes on the other side. Cut into wedges and serve with extra salsa.

ORZO RISOTTO
WITH PANCETTA & PEAS

3¾ cups hot chicken or
 vegetable stock or broth
12 oz orzo pasta
a pat of butter
1 teaspoon chopped garlic
5 oz diced pancetta
1⅓ cups shelled fresh peas
handful of parsley, chopped
1 cup grated Parmesan cheese
salt and black pepper

Serves **4**
Prep time **5**
Cooking time **10-15 minutes**

1 Put the stock or broth into a saucepan, bring to a boil, and add the pasta.

2 Meanwhile, melt the butter in a small skillet until foaming, add the garlic and pancetta, and cook for 2 minutes, or until the pancetta is crispy.

3 Add the pancetta and garlic to the orzo with the peas and continue to cook over medium heat for about 7 minutes, or until the pasta and peas are just tender, stirring occasionally to prevent the pasta from sticking and adding a little more water, if necessary.

4 Season with salt and black pepper and stir in the parsley and most of the Parmesan. Serve immediately, sprinkled with the remaining Parmesan and black pepper.

SIDES, SALADS, SAUCES, & SNACKS

180 SARDINES ON RYE

181 SPICED MACKEREL FILLETS

182 EGGS FLORENTINE

184 SMOKED MACKEREL PASTA SALAD

185 SEARED TUNA WITH BEAN & ARUGULA SALAD

186 HERBED LAMB WITH FIG SALAD

188 CYPRIOT CHICKEN & CHEESE SALAD

189 CHICKPEA & HERB SALAD

190 ORANGE & AVOCADO SALAD

192 RIBBONED CARROT SALAD

193 GRILLED HALLOUMI WITH WARM COUSCOUS SALAD

194 EGG, BASIL, & CHEESE SALAD WITH CHERRY TOMATOES

195 SPICY SWEET POTATO & FETA SALAD

196 REAL GUACAMOLE WITH RAW VEGETABLES

198 WARM ZUCCHINI & LIME SALAD

199 BEER FLAT BREADS WITH CHEESE & ONIONS

200 CORN FLAT BREADS WITH CORN & GRUYÈRE

201 BALSAMIC BRAISED LEEKS & BELL PEPPERS

202 MUSTARD & THYME SWEET POTATOES

203 FIRE-BAKED NEW POTATOES WITH GREEN DRESSING

204 BALSAMIC-ROASTED TOMATOES

204 ROASTED RED ONIONS

205 PANZANELLA

206 CRUSHED MINTED PEAS

206 GARLIC BREAD

207 DEVILED MUSHROOMS

208 TABBOULEH WITH FRUIT & NUTS

210 GREEN COUSCOUS WITH SPICED FRUIT SAUCE

GRILLED HALLOUMI & WARM
COUSCOUS SALAD

PANZANELLA

REAL GUACAMOLE

Sardines
ON RYE

2 (3¾ oz) cans sardines in oil, drained
½ cup cream cheese
2 tablespoons grated cucumber, drained
1 scallion, finely chopped
6 thin slices of rye bread
butter, for spreading
lettuce leaves

1 Put the sardines and cream cheese into a bowl and mash together. Stir in the cucumber and scallion.

2 Spread 3 slices of the rye bread with butter, add the sardine mixture and lettuce, and top with the remaining bread.

Serves **3**
Prep time **10 minutes**

CAMPING TIP

If you know you'll be arriving on site fairly late, bring a prepared meal that can be simply heated and served on the first night—setting up camp always takes longer than you think, and you'll be tired and hungry by the time the tent is erected.

SPICED
Mackerel Fillets

1 Mix together the oil, paprika, and cayenne in a bowl and season with salt and black pepper. Make 3 shallow cuts in the skin of each mackerel fillet and brush all over with the spiced oil.

2 Cook the lime quarters and mackerel fillets on a grill rack over a hot barbecue grill or campfire, skin side down, for about 5 minutes, or until the skin is crispy and the limes are charred. Turn the fish over and cook for another 1 minute, or until cooked through. Serve with an arugula salad.

2 tablespoons olive oil
1 tablespoon smoked paprika
1 teaspoon cayenne pepper
8 fresh mackerel fillets
2 limes, quartered
salt and black pepper
arugula salad, to serve

Serves 4
Prep time 5 minutes
Cooking time 6 minutes

EGGS Florentine

a pat of butter, plus extra for
  spreading
1 (6 oz) package fresh spinach
4 English muffins
3 tablespoons chopped parsley
1 cup hollandaise sauce
salt and black pepper
4 eggs
1 tablespoon distilled
  white vinegar

Serves 4
Prep time **10 minutes**
Cooking time **10 minutes**

1 Melt the butter in a large saucepan, add the spinach, and cook over medium heat, stirring, for 1–2 minutes, until wilted. Season with salt and black pepper, cover with a lid, and keep warm.

2 Halve the English muffins and toast, cut side down, in a ridged grill pan or over a barbecue grill or campfire until lightly charred. Wrap in a clean dish towel and keep warm. Mix the parsley and hollandaise sauce together in a bowl.

3 Meanwhile, bring a large saucepan of water to a boil. Break 1 of the eggs into a cup, making sure not to break the yolk. Add the vinegar to the boiling water, then stir the water rapidly in a circular motion to make a whirlpool. Carefully slide the egg into the center of the pan while the water is still swirling, holding the cup as close to the water as you can. Cook for 1–2 minutes, or until the white is firm and the yolk is soft, then lift out with a slotted spoon.

4 Butter 2 halves of an English muffin, then add one-quarter of the spinach and top with an egg. Spoon the hollandaise sauce over the egg and serve with black pepper.

5 Cook and serve the other 3 eggs in the same way, swirling a boiling water into a whirlpool each time before sliding in the egg.

SMOKED MACKEREL
PASTA SALAD

1 Cook the pasta in a large saucepan of lightly salted boiling water for 10-12 minutes, or according to package directions, until just tender. Drain and let cool.

2 Meanwhile, cook the beans in a saucepan of lightly salted boiling water for about 5 minutes, or until just tender. Drain and let cool.

3 To make the dressing, mix together all the ingredients in a small bowl and season with salt and black pepper.

4 Transfer the pasta to a large bowl, then flake the smoked mackerel fillets into the bowl. Add the leafy greens, cucumber, scallions, and cooled beans, then toss with some of the dressing.

5 Divide the pasta salad among serving bowls and top with the hard-boiled eggs. Serve with the dressing.

12 oz dried conchiglie pasta
2 cups green beans
4 hot-smoked peppered boneless mackerel fillets
4 cups mixed leafy greens, such as arugula, mâche, and mizuna
½ cucumber, cut in half lengthwise, seeded and cut into chunky pieces
2 scallions, finely sliced
2 hard-boiled eggs, quartered

Dressing
½ cup sour cream
1 tablespoon whole-grain mustard
1 teaspoon French mustard
2 tablespoons lemon juice
1 teaspoon chopped dill
1 teaspoon chopped tarragon
salt and black pepper

Serves 4
Prep time 20 minutes, plus cooling
Cooking time 10-12 minutes

SEARED TUNA
WITH **BEAN & ARUGULA SALAD**

1 Rub 1 tablespoon of the oil over the tuna steaks and season well with salt and black pepper. Heat a ridged grill pan until smoking hot, then cook the tuna for 1-2 minutes on each side, or until charred on the outside but still pink in the middle. Alternatively, cook for a little less or longer until cooked to your preference.

2 Meanwhile, mix 2 tablespoons of the lemon juice with the remaining oil in a bowl and season with salt and black pepper. Toss with the remaining ingredients in a large bowl and add more lemon juice to taste.

3 Serve the bean salad with the seared tuna.

¼ cup olive oil
4 tuna steaks (about 5 oz each)
2-4 tablespoons lemon juice
finely grated zest of ½ lemon
2 (13 oz) cans cannellini beans, drained
3½ cups arugula leaves
1 small red onion, finely sliced
1 red chile, seeded and chopped
salt and black pepper

Serves **4**
Prep time **10 minutes**
Cooking time **2-4 minutes**

Herbed Lamb
WITH FIG SALAD

2 tablespoons coriander seeds
2 tablespoons chopped
  rosemary
grated zest of 1 lemon
salt and black pepper
½ cup olive oil
1 garlic clove, crushed
12 lamb cutlets
4 cups arugula
4 figs, sliced
¾ cup pitted black ripe olives,
  halved
2-3 teaspoons lemon juice,
  to taste
yogurt, to serve

Serves 4
Prep time **15 minutes,**
plus marinating
Cooking time **4-6 minutes**

1 To make the rub, dry-fry the coriander seeds in a skillet over high heat for 2-3 minutes, until they begin to pop and release their aroma. Cool the coriander seeds and mix with the rosemary, lemon zest, and some salt and black pepper.

2 Put 2 tablespoons of the oil, the rub, the garlic, and some salt and black pepper into a large sealable plastic bag. Add the lamb, toss well, and seal the bag. Let marinate in a cooler for 1-4 hours.

3 Remove the lamb from the marinade and pat dry. Transfer to a grill rack over a hot barbecue grill or campfire and cook for 2-3 minutes on each side, or until cooked to your preference, then wrap loosely with aluminum foil and let rest for 5 minutes.

4 Meanwhile, to make the salad, put the arugula, figs, and olives in a large bowl and mix well. Whisk together the remaining oil and 2-3 teaspoons lemon juice with some salt and black pepper. Add to the salad and stir to coat the leaves. Serve with the lamb and some yogurt.

CYPRIOT CHICKEN
& Cheese Salad

3 boneless, skinless chicken
  breasts (about 4 oz each)
1 bunch of oregano, chopped
1 tablespoon olive oil
8 oz halloumi or Muenster
  cheese
salt and black pepper

Cypriot salad
1 cucumber, skinned, seeded,
  and cut lengthwise into
  short batons
4 beefsteak tomatoes, skinned,
  seeded, and cut into wedges
1 red onion, finely chopped
1 bunch of flat leaf parsley,
  coarsely chopped
3 tablespoons olive oil
1 tablespoon wine vinegar

Serves **4**
Prep time **20 minutes,
plus marinating**
Cooking time **about
25 minutes**

1 Put the chicken in a bowl, add the chopped oregano, olive oil, and salt and black pepper, and toss together. Cover with plastic wrap and let marinate in a cooler for 2 hours.

2 Transfer the chicken to a grill rack over a hot barbecue grill or campfire and cook for 6-8 minutes on each side, or until cooked through. Transfer to a plate, cut into chunks, cover with aluminum foil, and keep warm.

3 Meanwhile, to make the salad, put the cucumber, tomato wedges, chopped red onion, and parsley into a bowl. Add the olive oil and wine vinegar, toss well, and season with salt and black pepper.

4 Slice the halloumi or Muenster cheese into 8, then transfer to the grill rack and cook for 3-4 minutes on each side. Serve with the chicken and salad.

CHICKPEA & HERB SALAD

1 Put the bulgur wheat in a heatproof bowl and cover with boiling water. Let stand until the water is absorbed, then drain well, pressing out as much moisture as possible with the back of a spoon. Let cool.

2 Mix together the oil, lemon juice, parsley, mint, and salt and black pepper in a large bowl. Add the chickpeas, tomatoes, onion, cucumber, and bulgur wheat. Mix well, then add the feta, stirring lightly to avoid breaking up the cheese.

3/4 cup bulgur wheat
1/4 cup olive oil
1 tablespoon lemon juice
2 tablespoons chopped
   flat leaf parsley
1 tablespoon chopped mint
1 (15 oz) can chickpeas, drained
8 cherry tomatoes, halved
1 tablespoon chopped onion
1 cup diced cucumber
1 cup diced feta cheese
salt and black pepper

Serves **4**
Prep time **20 minutes,
plus standing and cooling**

ORANGE
& AVOCADO SALAD

4 large juicy oranges
2 small ripe avocados, peeled
 and pitted
2 teaspoons cardamom pods
3 tablespoons olive oil
1 tablespoon honey
pinch of ground allspice
2 teaspoons lemon juice
salt and black pepper
sprigs of watercress or other
 peppery greens, to garnish

Serves 4
Prep time **15 minutes**

1 Using a sharp knife, remove the peel and pith from the oranges. Working over a bowl to catch the juice, cut between the membranes to remove the segments. Slice the avocados and toss gently with the orange segments. Pile into serving bowls.

2 Reserve a few whole cardamom pods for garnishing. Crush the remainder, using a mortar and pestle, to extract the seeds or place them in a small bowl and crush with the end of a rolling pin. Pick out and discard the pods.

3 Mix the seeds with the oil, honey, allspice, and lemon juice in a bowl. Season with salt and black pepper and stir in the reserved orange juice.

4 Garnish the salads with sprigs of watercress or other peppery greens and the reserved cardamom pods and serve with the dressing spooned over the top.

RIBBONED CARROT *Salad*

4 carrots
2 celery sticks
1 bunch of scallions
¼ cup olive oil
2 tablespoons lime juice
2 teaspoons sugar
¼ teaspoon dried red pepper
   flakes
2 tablespoons chopped mint
⅓ cup salted peanuts
salt and black pepper

Serves 4
Prep time **15 minutes,
plus soaking**

1 Fill a medium bowl halfway with cold water, adding a few
  ice cubes, if possible.

2 Scrub the carrots and pare off as many long ribbons as
  you can from each. Place the ribbons in the water. Cut
the celery into 2 inch lengths. Cut each length into thin slices.
Cut the scallions into 2 inch lengths and shred lengthwise.
Add the celery and scallions to the water and let soak for
15-20 minutes, until the vegetables curl up.

3 Mix together the oil, lime juice, sugar, dried red pepper
  flakes, and mint in a small bowl and season with salt and
black pepper.

4 Thoroughly drain the vegetables and toss in a bowl with
  the dressing, peanuts, and salt and black pepper. Serve
the salad immediately.

GRILLED HALLOUMI
with Warm Couscous Salad

1 Heat 3 tablespoons of the oil in a skillet, add the onions and two-thirds of the chile, and cook over medium heat, stirring, for about 5 minutes, until softened. Add the chickpeas and tomatoes and cook over high heat for 3 minutes, stirring occasionally, until the chickpeas are heated through and the tomatoes are softened but still retaining their shape.

2 Meanwhile, put the couscous in a heatproof bowl, add enough boiling water to cover by ½ inch, and mix in the salt. Cover with plastic wrap and let stand for 5 minutes, then fluff up with a fork.

3 Heat a ridged grill pan until hot. Mix the remaining olive oil and chile with the herbs in a shallow bowl. Add the halloumi or Muenster cheese slices and toss to coat, then transfer to the ridged grill pan and cook for 2–3 minutes, turning once, until browned in places.

4 Stir the couscous into the chickpea mixture and cook for 1 minute to heat through. Pile onto plates and top with the cheese slices.

⅓ cup olive oil
2 red onions, thinly sliced
1 red chile, coarsely chopped
1 (15 oz) can chickpeas, drained
10 cherry tomatoes, halved
1 cup couscous
½ teaspoon salt
3 tablespoons chopped parsley
1 tablespoon thyme leaves
12 oz halloumi or Muenster cheese, thickly sliced

Serves **4**
Prep time **10 minutes**
Cooking time **10 minutes**

EGG, BASIL, & CHEESE
SALAD WITH CHERRY TOMATOES

2 tablespoons olive oil
2 eggs, beaten
2 handfuls of basil, coarsely
  chopped
1⅓ cups crumbled feta cheese
16 cherry plum tomatoes,
  halved
3 cups watercress or other
  peppery greens
1 tablespoon balsamic vinegar
black pepper

Serves **4**
Prep time **10 minutes**
Cooking time **2 minutes**

1 Heat 1 tablespoon of the oil in a skillet and swirl around. Beat the eggs in a large bowl with the basil and plenty of black pepper, then pour into the pan in a thin layer and cook for about 2 minutes, or until golden and set. Remove and cut into thick strips.

2 Meanwhile, toss the feta, cherry tomatoes, and watercress or other peppery greens in a bowl. Mix the remaining oil with the balsamic vinegar, pour the dressing over the salad, and toss to coat.

3 Add the omelet strips, toss to mix, and serve while still warm.

Spicy SWEET POTATO & FETA SALAD

1 Heat a ridged grill pan until hot. Toss together 2 tablespoons of the oil and the sweet potatoes in a bowl. Season well with salt and black pepper, then cook in the hot ridged grill pan for about 3 minutes on each side, or until tender and lightly charred.

2 Meanwhile, mix together the remaining oil and vinegar in a bowl and season with salt and black pepper. Add the spinach and onion and toss together.

3 Transfer the sweet potatoes to plates, top with the spinach-and-onion mixture, feta, chile, and olives, and serve.

⅓ cup olive oil
2 sweet potatoes, thinly sliced
1 tablespoon white wine vinegar
5 cups fresh baby spinach
1 tablespoon finely chopped
   red onion
1 cup crumbled feta cheese
1 red chile, sliced
⅓ cup pitted black ripe olives
salt and black pepper

Serves 4
Prep time **10 minutes**
Cooking time **about 6 minutes**

REAL GUACAMOLE
with raw vegetables

2 large firm, ripe avocados
½ small red onion, finely
  chopped
2 tablespoons lime juice
3 tablespoons finely chopped
  fresh cilantro
¼ teaspoon garlic powder
¼ teaspoon celery salt
pinch of cayenne pepper
½ teaspoon paprika
3 tomatoes, seeded and
  finely chopped
few dashes of Tabasco
  (optional)
salt and black pepper

To serve
6 carrots, cut into batons
3 cups cauliflower florets
4 celery sticks, cut into batons
8 oz radishes, trimmed
8 baby corn

Serves **4**
Prep time **15 minutes**

1 Peel the avocados and remove the pits, then mash the flesh in a small bowl with the back of a fork to break it up.

2 Add the red onion, lime juice, cilantro, garlic powder, celery salt, and spices. Mix until almost smooth, with some small lumps, then season with salt and black pepper. Stir in the tomatoes and add the Tabasco, if using.

3 Arrange the raw vegetables on a large plate and serve with the guacamole.

WARM
ZUCCHINI &
Lime Salad

1 tablespoon olive oil
grated zest and juice of 1 lime
1 garlic clove, finely chopped
2 tablespoons coarsely chopped
   fresh cilantro, plus extra to
   garnish
2 zucchini, cut into thin
   diagonal slices
salt and black pepper

Serves 4
Prep time 10 minutes
Cooking time 10 minutes

1 Mix together the oil, lime zest and juice, garlic, chopped cilantro, and salt and black pepper in a sealable plastic bag. Add the zucchini slices and toss in the oil mixture. Seal and set aside until ready to cook.

2 Heat a ridged grill pan until hot. Arrange as many zucchini slices as will fit in a single layer over the bottom of the pan and cook for 2–3 minutes, or until browned on the underside. Turn the slices over and brown on the other side. Transfer the slices to a serving dish, cover with aluminum foil, and keep warm. Repeat with the remaining zucchini.

3 Pour any remaining dressing over the zucchini, sprinkle with a little extra chopped cilantro to garnish, and serve immediately.

BEER FLAT BREADS
WITH CHEESE & ONIONS

1 Put the flour, salt, yeast, 3 tablespoons of the oil, and the mustard into a bowl and stir in the ale. Mix with a blunt knife to make a soft dough, adding a little more ale or water if the dough is dry. Turn out onto a lightly floured board and knead for about 10 minutes, until the dough is smooth and elastic. (If you've no surface to work on, work the dough in the bowl as best as you can.) Return the dough to the bowl, cover with a dish towel or plastic wrap, and let rest in a warm place (near the fire if already lit) until the dough has doubled in size.

2 Meanwhile, heat the remaining oil in a skillet, add the onions, and sauté over low heat for about 15 minutes, stirring frequently, until soft and deep golden. Let cool.

3 Divide the dough into 12 pieces and roll out each on a floured board to a circle about 6½ inches in diameter. Sprinkle the centers of 6 of the circles with cheese and spoon the onions on top. Brush the edges lightly with water and press another circle of dough on top so the filling is sandwiched. Flatten out with a rolling pin until the dough is so thin that the filling shows through.

4 Heat a large, dry skillet or ridged grill pan, add 1 bread, and cook until pale golden on the underside. Flip the bread over and cook on the other side until the dough is cooked through, 5-7 minutes in total. Wrap in aluminum foil and keep warm. Repeat with the remaining breads.

2¼ cups white bread flour, plus extra for dusting
1 teaspoon salt
1 teaspoon active dry yeast
¼ cup olive oil
2 teaspoons Dijon mustard
⅔ cup strong ale
2 onions, chopped
1 cup shredded cheddar or Gruyère cheese

Serves 6
Prep time **30 minutes, plus rising**
Cooking time **45-55 minutes**

CORN FLAT BREADS
WITH CORN & GRUYÈRE

¾ cup plus 2 tablespoons
masa harina flour
¾ cup plus 2 tablespoons
all-purpose flour, plus extra
for dusting
1 teaspoon baking powder
1 teaspoon salt
2 tablespoons olive oil

Topping
1¼ cups shredded Gruyère
cheese
¾ cup drained canned
corn kernels
4 tomatoes, thinly sliced
1 small butterhead lettuce,
shredded
sweet chili sauce
sour cream

Serves 4
Prep time **20 minutes**
Cooking time **25-40 minutes**

1 Put the flours, baking powder, salt, and olive oil into a bowl and stir in ⅔ cup of cold water to make a soft dough. Divide the dough into 4 even pieces and roll out each as thinly as possible on a well-floured board to circles about 8 inches in diameter.

2 Heat a dry skillet for 5 minutes, add 1 flat bread, and cook for 2-4 minutes on each side, until pale golden and cooked through. Slide out of the pan onto a sheet of aluminum foil and keep warm. Repeat with the remaining flat breads.

3 To heat through and serve, sprinkle a thin layer of cheese and corn over a flat bread and add several slices of tomato. Return to the stove or fire, either in the pan or on a sheet of foil, and heat through until the cheese starts to melt.

4 Sprinkle with shredded lettuce, drizzle with chili sauce and a little sour cream, and fold or roll up to serve.

5 Repeat with the remaining flat breads and toppings.

CAMPING TIP

When you're drinking in your tent, a shoe makes a good glass or mug holder that will help avoid spillages and soggy sleeping bags.

BALSAMIC
Braised
Leeks
& BELL PEPPERS

2 tablespoons olive oil
2 leeks, trimmed and cut into
  ½ inch pieces
1 orange bell pepper, cored,
  seeded and cut into ½ inch
  chunks
1 red bell pepper, cored,
  seeded, and cut into ½ inch
  chunks
3 tablespoons balsamic
  vinegar
handful of flat leaf parsley,
  chopped
salt and black pepper

Serves 4
Prep time 5 minutes
Cooking time 20 minutes

1 Heat the oil in a saucepan, add the leeks and bell peppers, and stir well. Cover with a lid and cook gently for 10 minutes.

2 Add the balsamic vinegar and cook, uncovered, for another 10 minutes. The vegetables should be brown from the vinegar and all the liquid should have evaporated. Season well with salt and black pepper, then stir in the chopped parsley just before serving.

Mustard & Thyme SWEET POTATOES

6 large sweet potatoes (about 8 oz each), scrubbed

Mustard and thyme butter
1 stick (¼ lb) butter, softened
1 tablespoon whole-grain mustard
1 teaspoon chopped thyme
black pepper

Serves **6**
Prep time **5 minutes**
Cooking time **40 minutes**

1 Wrap each potato in a double layer of aluminum foil, then tuck between hot coals or logs, allowing some of the coals or logs to cover the potatoes. Cook for about 40 minutes, or until tender, rotating the packages several times during cooking.

2 Meanwhile, to make the mustard and thyme butter, put the butter, mustard, thyme, and some black pepper into a bowl and mash with a fork until evenly mixed. Set aside.

3 Carefully remove the potatoes from the foil packages. Cut in half and serve topped with the butter.

FIRE-BAKED NEW
POTATOES
with green dressing

1 Put the potatoes onto a large square of heavy-duty aluminum foil. Drizzle with 1 tablespoon of the oil and season with salt and black pepper. Bring the foil up around the potatoes and seal well, then tuck the package between hot coals or logs to cook. This will take 1-2 hours, depending on the intensity of the fire. Rotate the package several times during cooking so the potatoes cook evenly.

2 Mix together the herbs, capers, remaining oil, lemon juice, honey, and a little salt and black pepper in a small bowl.

3 Carefully unwrap the foil and spoon the dressing over the potatoes to serve.

1 lb new potatoes, scrubbed and rinsed
½ cup olive oil
large handful each of parsley and chives, chopped
2 tablespoons chopped mint
2 tablespoons capers, drained and chopped
1 tablespoon lemon juice
2 teaspoons honey
salt and black pepper

Serves **4**
Prep time **10 minutes**
Cooking time **1-2 hours**

BALSAMIC-ROASTED
TOMATOES

1 Put the tomatoes, cut side up, onto a large piece of heavy-duty aluminum foil and drizzle with the oil and vinegar. Tear half the basil over the top, add the pine nuts, and season with salt and black pepper.

2 Bring the foil up around the tomatoes and seal well, then tuck between hot coals or logs to cook for 30-40 minutes, or until softened. Rotate the package several times during cooking.

3 Toast the bread, cut side down, on a rack over the barbecue grill or campfire, until charred.

4 Carefully unwrap the foil and spoon the tomatoes onto the toast. Sprinkle with the remaining basil leaves and serve immediately.

12 plum tomatoes, halved
2 tablespoons olive oil
2 teaspoons balsamic vinegar
1 small bunch of basil
2 tablespoons pine nuts
4 slices of ciabatta bread
salt and black pepper

Serves 4
Prep time **10 minutes**
Cooking time **30-40 minutes**

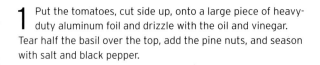

Roasted RED ONIONS

handful each of bay leaves
 and thyme
8 small red onions, peeled
2 tablespoons olive oil
3 tablespoons balsamic glaze
salt and black pepper

Serves 4
Prep time **10 minutes**
Cooking time **1-1½ hours**

1 Sprinkle the herbs onto a large piece of heavy-duty aluminum foil and put the onions on top. Drizzle with the oil and season lightly with salt and black pepper.

2 Bring the foil up around the onions and seal well, then tuck between hot coals or logs to cook for 40-50 minutes, or until softened.

3 Carefully unwrap the foil and drizzle the onions with the balsamic glaze. Reseal the package and return to the fire until the onions are soft.

PANZANELLA

ORIGINATING FROM TUSCANY, ITALY, THIS IS A POPULAR SUMMER DISH, WITH THE TOASTED BREAD SOAKING UP THE JUICES FROM THE TOMATOES AND OLIVE OIL AND VINEGAR DRESSING. THE RIPER THE TOMATOES, THE MORE JUICE THERE WILL BE, AND THE MORE DELICIOUS THE DISH.

4 slices of ciabatta bread
4 ripe tomatoes, cored and
  chopped
½ cucumber, seeded, peeled,
  and cubed
1 red onion, chopped
handful of chopped
  flat leaf parsley
1 tablespoon chopped pitted
  black ripe olives
¼ cup olive oil
1-2 tablespoons wine vinegar
juice of ½ lemon
salt and black pepper

Serves 4
Prep time **15 minutes,
plus standing**
Cooking time **5 minutes**

1 Toast the bread lightly in a ridged grill pan or on a rack over a barbecue grill or campfire, then tear into pieces and put into a large bowl. Add the tomatoes, cucumber, onion, parsley, and olives.

2 Mix together the oil, vinegar, and lemon juice in a bowl and season with salt and black pepper.

3 Pour the dressing over the salad and mix well. Cover and let stand for at least 1 hour to let the flavors mingle.

CRUSHED MINTED PEAS

A COMPULSORY ACCOMPANIMENT FOR SERVING WITH FISH OR LAMB, THESE MINTED PEAS ARE CRUSHED WITH A LITTLE CRÈME FRAÎCHE AND BUTTER TO PRODUCE A PERFECT SIDE DISH.

3 cups shelled fresh peas
several sprigs of mint
2 tablespoons butter
2 tablespoons crème fraîche
  or Greek yogurt
salt and black pepper

Serves 4-6
Prep time 10 minutes
Cooking time 5 minutes

1 Cook the peas with the mint in a large saucepan of boiling water for about 5 minutes, or until tender. Drain and return to the pan, discarding the mint.

2 Stir in the butter and crème fraîche or yogurt and use a fork to crush the peas coarsely. Season with salt and black pepper and reheat gently.

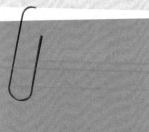

GARLIC BREAD

4 tablespoons butter, softened
1 garlic clove, crushed
2 tablespoons thyme leaves,
  coarsely chopped (optional)
1 white or whole wheat baguette
  or long, thin Italian bread
salt and black pepper

Serves 4
Prep time 10 minutes
Cooking time about 15 minutes

1 Beat the softened butter with the garlic and thyme, if using, in a bowl and season with a little salt and black pepper. Cut the bread into thick slices, almost all the way through but leaving attached at the bottom. Spread the butter thickly over each slice.

2 Wrap the bread in aluminum foil and cook on a grill rack over a barbecue grill or campfire for about 15 minutes, turning the package occasionally. Alternatively, cook in a ridged grill pan on a camping stove.

Deviled
MUSHROOMS

1 Finely chop the scallions, reserving the green tops. Heat the butter and oil in a skillet, add the white chopped scallions and the mushrooms, and sauté, stirring, for 3-4 minutes, or until golden.

2 Stir in the Worcestershire sauce, mustard, and tomato paste. Add ¼ cup of water, the Tabasco, if using, and a little salt and black pepper and cook for 2 minutes, stirring, until the sauce is beginning to thicken.

3 Meanwhile, toast the bread on both sides in a ridged grill pan or on a rack over a barbecue grill or campfire. Transfer to plates.

4 Stir the green scallion tops through the mushrooms and cook for 1 minute, then spoon over the toast and serve.

6 scallions
4 tablespoons butter
1 tablespoon sunflower oil
6 cups sliced white mushrooms
  (about 1 lb)
2 tablespoons Worcestershire
  sauce
2 teaspoons whole-grain
  mustard
2 teaspoons tomato paste
a few drops of Tabasco sauce
  (optional)
4 slices of crusty bread
salt and black pepper

Serves 4
Prep time **5 minutes**
Cooking time **10 minutes**

TABBOULEH
WITH FRUIT & NUTS

1 cup bulgur wheat
½ cup unsalted, shelled
   pistachio nuts
1 small red onion, finely
   chopped
3 garlic cloves, crushed
2 handfuls of flat leaf parsley,
   chopped
large handful of mint, chopped
finely grated zest and juice of
   1 lemon or lime
1 cup sliced prunes
¼ cup olive oil
salt and black pepper

1 Put the bulgur wheat into a heatproof bowl and cover with plenty of boiling water. Let stand for 15 minutes.

2 Meanwhile, mix together the pistachios, onion, garlic, parsley, mint, lemon or lime zest and juice, and prunes in a large bowl.

3 Drain the bulgur wheat well, pressing out as much moisture as possible with the back of a spoon. Add to the other ingredients with the oil and toss together. Season with salt and black pepper and serve.

Serves **4**
Prep time **10 minutes,
plus standing**

Green Couscous
WITH SPICED
FRUIT SAUCE

2 cups hot vegetable stock
   or broth
1½ cups couscous
½ cup unsalted, shelled
   pistachio nuts, coarsely
   chopped
2 scallions, chopped
small handful of parsley,
   chopped
1 (15 oz) can great Northern
   beans, drained
salt and black pepper

Spiced fruit sauce
½ teaspoon saffron threads
1 tablespoon cardamom pods
2 teaspoons coriander seeds
½ teaspoon chili powder
¼ cup slivered almonds
⅔ cup finely chopped
   dried apricots

Serves **4**
Prep time **20 minutes,
plus standing**
Cooking time **2 minutes**

1 To make the sauce, put the saffron into a small cup and pour over 1 tablespoon boiling water. Let stand for 3 minutes.

2 Crush the cardamom pods using a mortar and pestle, or place the pods in a small bowl and crush with the end of a rolling pin. Pick out and discard the pods, then lightly crush the seeds.

3 Add the coriander seeds, chili powder, and almonds to the bowl and crush again. Stir in the apricots. Pour in the saffron and soaking liquid and 1 cup of the hot stock, season with salt and black pepper, and mix well. Transfer to a saucepan and heat through.

4 Meanwhile, put the couscous in a heatproof bowl and add the remaining hot stock. Cover with plastic wrap and let stand for 5 minutes, until the stock is absorbed, then fluff up with a fork. Stir in the pistachios, scallions, parsley, and beans and season with salt and black pepper. Serve with the fruit sauce.

Thai-Dressed
TOFU ROLLS

1 Remove 8 leaves from the lettuce. Fill a large heatproof bowl with boiling water. Add the separated leaves and let stand for 10 seconds. Rinse in cold water and drain well.

2 Finely shred the remaining lettuce and toss in a bowl with the tofu and snow peas.

3 Mix together the oil, soy sauce, lime juice, sugar, chile, garlic, and black pepper in a separate bowl and add to the tofu mixture. Toss together gently, using two spoons.

4 Spoon a little mixture onto the center of each blanched lettuce leaf, then roll up and serve.

1 small iceberg lettuce
9 oz tofu, diced
1½ cups shredded snow peas
  (shredded lengthwise)
2 tablespoons olive oil
2 tablespoons light soy sauce
2 tablespoons lime juice
1 tablespoon packed light
  brown sugar
1 Thai chile, seeded and sliced
1 garlic clove, crushed
black pepper

Serves 4
Prep time 15 minutes

TORTILLAS
with Chili & Eggplant Yogurt

1 Heat the oil in a skillet, add the eggplant, and sauté for about 10 minutes, until golden. Drain and let cool.

2 Mix together the herbs, chile, yogurt, and mayonnaise in a bowl and season with salt and black pepper.

3 Arrange the fried eggplant slices over the tortillas and spread with the Greek yogurt mixture, then top with the cucumber slices. Roll up each tortilla, sprinkle with paprika, and serve.

¼ cup olive oil
1 eggplant, thinly sliced
small handful of mint, chopped
small handful of parsley, chopped
2 tablespoons chopped chives
1 green chile, seeded and thinly sliced
1 cup Greek yogurt
2 tablespoons mayonnaise
2 large tortillas
3 inch length of cucumber, thinly sliced
salt and black pepper
paprika, to garnish

Serves **2**
Prep time **10 minutes,**
plus cooling
Cooking time **10 minutes**

CAMPING TIP

It doesn't take much moisture to ruin a roll of toilet paper—keep them in sealable plastic containers or zip-top bags so they stay dry. Alternatively, hang them up on the inside of the tent for easy access— and just take what you need.

BEAN & RED PEPPER *Burritos*

3 red bell peppers, cored, seeded, and cut into small chunks
1 (15 oz) can black beans, drained
½ bunch of scallions, chopped
¼ cup chopped fresh cilantro
1 tablespoon hot pepper sauce
1 cup shredded cheddar cheese
4 large tortilla wraps
salt

Serves 4
Prep time 15 minutes
Cooking time 35-45 mins

1 Heat a skillet, add the bell peppers, and cook for about 15 minutes, or until softened and lightly browned.

2 Put the bell peppers into a bowl and add the beans, scallions, cilantro, and pepper sauce. Mix well. Stir in the cheese and a little salt.

3 Spoon the mixture onto the centers of the tortilla wraps. Spread the filling out into a strip that comes about 1½ inches from the edges. Fold these edges over, then roll up each tortilla, starting from an unfolded end, to enclose the filling.

4 Wrap each tortilla in heavy-duty aluminum foil, then tuck the packages between hot coals or logs to cook for 20-30 minutes, until cooked through, turning the packages occasionally so they cook evenly.

CAMPING TIP

Take a thin doormat to place by the tent door so you don't traipse too much water and mud inside. If you don't have a doormat—or you're short of space — you could use a mat from the car.

Sweet Potato, BACON & THYME CAKES

1 Cook the sweet potato in a saucepan of boiling water for about 5 minutes, or until soft. Drain well, then return to the pan and mash well. Transfer to a bowl.

2 Meanwhile, heat 1 tablespoon of the oil in a skillet, add the diced bacon, and fry until crisp. Using a slotted spoon, add to the sweet potato, reserving the oil in the pan.

3 Add the thyme, egg, and buttermilk to the sweet potato mixture and beat together to make a smooth batter. Add the flour and stir until evenly mixed.

4 Reheat the skillet until hot. Scoop large spoonfuls of the mixture into the pan, spacing them slightly apart, and cook until golden on the underside, then turn the cakes over and cook on the other side until golden and cooked through. Remove from the pan and serve warm, drizzled with maple syrup or chili sauce.

5 Repeat with the remaining mixture, adding a little more oil to the pan as required.

1 large sweet potato, cut into small chunks
1-2 tablespoons vegetable oil
4 oz bacon, finely diced
1 tablespoon chopped thyme
1 egg
2/3 cup buttermilk
1 1/3 cups all-purpose flour
1 1/4 teaspoons baking powder
maple syrup or sweet chili sauce, to serve

Serves 4
Prep time **15 minutes**
Cooking time **20-30 minutes**

5 WAYS WITH ...

Make the most of some traditional and versatile camping ingredients with these quick, easy, and delicious meals and snacks, and you'll never be without a bite to eat.

EGGS

1 You can't beat a bacon and egg roll for a classic camping breakfast. Cook the bacon and eggs together in one large skillet and serve between thick bread slices in bread rolls.

2 Soft-boiled egg dippers can be served with strips of toast or breadsticks, or try with steamed asparagus for a grown-up treat.

3 Scrambled eggs served in croissants, English muffins, or wraps make a fuss-free meal.

4 Frittatas are easy to cook when camping and they're a great way of using up any leftover vegetables on the last day.

5 Huevos rancheros (ranch eggs) is the perfect camping recipe: fried onion, chile, garlic, bell peppers, and zucchini are fried with a can of tomatoes. Make a couple of wells in the mix, crack in 2 eggs, simmer until the eggs are cooked through, and serve with cilantro.

BAKED BEANS

1. Cook away the liquid until the sauce is thick and the beans are heavy. Add some shredded cheese and roll up the mixture in a wrap.

2. Cook a one-dish bean casserole with frankfurters, a dash of Worcestershire sauce, and a good dollop of mustard.

3. Add chile and any other spices to your beans and serve with baked potatoes or crusty bread.

4. Mash baked beans with boiled (and drained) potatoes and make patties to cook in a ridged grill pan or skillet over the campfire.

5. For a quick, filling and hassle-free meal, heat a can of beans, cook some pasta, and combine the two ingredients.

CANNED TOMATOES

1. Reduce down a can of tomatoes—with a dash of balsamic, some garlic, and basil, if you have them—and use as a "pizza" topping on pita bread, halved baguettes, or wraps.

2. Add a dash of Worcestershire sauce and serve the tomatoes on toast.

3. Make a ratatouille with sautéed onion, bell peppers, and a can of tomatoes and serve with baked potatoes, meat, or rice. It also tastes great served cold, so it's perfect for a lunch of leftovers.

4. Add a can of drained kidney beans (and zucchini or red bell pepper if you have them) and a pinch of dried chile or dried red pepper flakes to a can of tomatoes and simmer for 10 minutes for a quick and easy vegetarian chili.

5. Make a hearty soup or stew with canned tomatoes and any meat or vegetables you have in the camping pantry. You could also add a handful of cooked rice or pasta for a more substantial meal.

FRESH TOMATO SAUCE

1 Put the tomatoes into a heatproof bowl, cover with boiling water, and let stand for about 2 minutes, or until the skins start to split. Pour away the water. Peel and coarsely chop the tomatoes.

2 Heat the oil in a large saucepan, add the onion, and sauté over medium heat for about 5 minutes, until softened but not browned. Add the garlic and sauté for another 1 minute.

3 Add the tomatoes and cook for 20-25 minutes, stirring frequently, until the sauce is thickened and pulpy.

4 Stir in the oregano and season with salt and black pepper. If the sauce is tart, add a sprinkling of sugar.

8 ripe, full-flavored tomatoes (about 2 lb)
½ cup olive oil
1 onion, finely chopped
2 garlic cloves, crushed
2 tablespoons chopped oregano
sprinkling of sugar (optional)
salt and black pepper

Serves **4**
Prep time **15 minutes**
Cooking time **30 minutes**

Chasseur SAUCE

3 tablespoons butter
3 cups thinly sliced white mushrooms
2 shallots, finely chopped
2 teaspoons all-purpose flour
⅔ cup dry white wine
1¼ cups beef or chicken stock or broth
2 tablespoons finely chopped chervil or tarragon
1 tablespoon brandy (optional)
salt and black pepper

Serves **4**
Prep time **10 minutes**
Cooking time **25 minutes**

1 Melt the butter in a large saucepan until foaming, add the mushrooms and shallots, and cook for 5 minutes, until lightly browned. Transfer the mushrooms to a plate with a slotted spoon, leaving any small pieces of shallot in the pan.

2 Add the flour to the pan and cook for 2 minutes, stirring constantly, until it begins to darken. Remove from the heat and gradually blend in the wine, then the stock or broth.

3 Return to the heat and bring to a boil, then simmer gently for 15 minutes, until the sauce is slightly thickened. Stir in the mushrooms, chervil or tarragon, brandy, if using, and salt and black pepper to taste. Serve hot.

AMATRICIANA
Sauce

THIS IS A GOOD CHOICE FOR THOSE WHO LIKE THEIR TOMATO SAUCE TO HAVE A PUNCHIER FLAVOR. IF THE TOMATOES ARE LACKING IN FLAVOR, STIR IN A GENEROUS DOLLOP OF TOMATO PASTE.

8 ripe, full-flavored tomatoes
  (about 2 lb)
⅓ cup olive oil
1 large onion, finely chopped
1 celery stick, finely chopped
3 oz pancetta or bacon, cubed
3 garlic cloves, crushed
1 hot red chile, seeded and
  finely chopped
salt and black pepper

Serves 4
Prep time **10 minutes**
Cooking time **40 minutes**

1 Put the tomatoes into a heatproof bowl, cover with boiling water, and let stand for about 2 minutes, or until the skins start to split. Pour away the water. Peel and coarsely chop the tomatoes.

2 Heat the oil in a large saucepan, add the onion, celery, and pancetta, and cook gently for 6–8 minutes, stirring frequently, until softened. Add the garlic and chile and cook for another 2 minutes.

3 Stir in the chopped tomatoes and cook gently, uncovered, for about 30 minutes, stirring frequently, or until the sauce is thick and pulpy. Season with salt and black pepper to taste and serve.

PUTTANESCA SAUCE

THIS INTENSE ITALIAN TOMATO SAUCE HAS PLENTY OF EXTRA FLAVORS, SUCH AS BLACK RIPE OLIVES, ANCHOVIES, AND CHILES. THICK AND RICH, IT'S GREAT TOSSED WITH ALMOST ANY PASTA, ESPECIALLY TYPES OF LONG PASTA.

1 Heat the oil in a large saucepan, add the onion, and sauté over medium heat for about 5 minutes, until softened. Add the garlic and chile and cook for another 1 minute.

2 Add the anchovy fillets, tomatoes, sugar, and olives and bring to a boil, then simmer gently for 10 minutes, until the sauce is thick.

3 Add the basil leaves, capers, and a little salt and heat through, stirring, for 1 minute. Serve hot, sprinkled with Parmesan cheese, if desired.

¼ cup olive oil
1 onion, finely chopped
3 garlic cloves, crushed
1 small red chile, seeded and
   finely chopped
6 anchovy fillets, chopped
2 (14½ oz) cans diced tomatoes
½ teaspoon sugar
¾ cup pitted and finely chopped
   black ripe olives
small handful of basil leaves
2 tablespoons capers, drained
salt
grated Parmesan cheese,
   to serve (optional)

Serves **4**
Prep time **15 minutes**
Cooking time **15 minutes**

Tomato & Mushroom SAUCE

1   Put the tomatoes into a heatproof bowl, cover with boiling water, and let stand for about 2 minutes, or until the skins start to split. Pour away the water. Peel and coarsely chop the tomatoes.

2   Heat the oil in a large saucepan, add the onion and garlic, and cook over low heat, stirring frequently, until the onion is soft. Add the tomatoes, oregano, and a little salt and black pepper.

3   Bring to a simmer, then cover with a lid and cook gently for about 10 minutes. Add the mushrooms and cook for another 5 minutes, until thickened and pulpy. Break up the tomatoes frequently during cooking.

4   Adjust the seasoning, if necessary, and serve immediately.

8 ripe, full-flavored tomatoes (about 2 lb)
1/3 cup olive oil
1 large onion, finely chopped
1 garlic clove, finely chopped
2 tablespoons chopped oregano
3 cups finely sliced cremini mushrooms
salt and black pepper

Serves 4-6
Prep time **15 minutes**
Cooking time **25 minutes**

BOLOGNESE SAUCE

2 tablespooons butter
2 tablespoons olive oil
1 onion, finely chopped
2 celery sticks, finely chopped
2 garlic cloves, crushed
1 lb ground round or ground
   sirloin beef
8 oz spicy Italian-style
   sausages, skins removed
1¼ cups red or white wine
1 (14½ oz) can diced tomatoes
1 teaspoon sugar
2 bay leaves
1 teaspoon dried oregano
2 tablespoons tomato paste
salt and black pepper

Serves 4-6
Prep time **15 minutes**
Cooking time **1¼ hours**

COMBINING ITALIAN-STYLE SPICY SAUSAGES WITH GROUND BEEF GIVES THIS SAUCE A RICH MEATY FLAVOR REMINISCENT OF THE TRADITIONAL SAUCE SERVED IN BOLOGNA, ITALY. ALLOW TIME FOR LONG, GENTLE COOKING TO TENDERIZE THE MEAT AND LET THE FLAVORS MINGLE.

1 Heat the butter and oil in a large saucepan, add the onion and celery, and cook over medium heat for about 5 minutes, until softened. Add the garlic, beef, and skinned sausages and cook until they are lightly browned, breaking up the beef and the sausages with a wooden spoon.

2 Add the wine and let simmer for 1-2 minutes, until slightly evaporated. Add the tomatoes, sugar, bay leaves, oregano, tomato paste, and a little salt and black pepper and bring just to a boil. Cover with a lid and cook over low heat for about 1 hour, stirring occasionally, until thick, pulpy, and cooked through.

CHORIZO CHERRY TOMATO SAUCE

ADDING PIECES OF SPICY CHORIZO SAUSAGE TO A TOMATO SAUCE IS ONE OF THE EASIEST AND TASTIEST WAYS OF GIVING IT PLENTY OF BOLD FLAVOR. THIS SAUCE IS DELICIOUS WITH ALMOST ANY WHITE FISH.

1 Heat the oil in a saucepan, add the onion, and sauté gently, stirring, for about 3 minutes, until beginning to soften. Add the chorizo and fennel or celery seeds and cook for another 2 minutes.

2 Strain the liquid from the can of tomatoes through a strainer into the pan, reserving the whole pieces. Add the vinegar, honey, and a little salt and black pepper to the pan and bring to a boil. Cover with a lid and cook over low heat for 8 minutes.

3 Add the strained tomatoes and adjust the seasoning, if necessary. Heat through for 1 minute and serve hot.

3 tablespoons olive oil
1 large red onion, finely chopped
4 oz chorizo sausage, finely diced
1 teaspoon fennel or celery seeds
1 (14½ oz) can cherry tomatoes
1 tablespoon wine vinegar
1 tablespoon honey
salt and black pepper

Serves 4
Prep time **10 minutes**
Cooking time **15 minutes**

SAUCE VIERGE

MIX THE SAUCE A COUPLE OF HOURS IN ADVANCE SO IT'S READY TO HEAT THROUGH GENTLY BEFORE SERVING.

1 Put the tomatoes in a heatproof bowl, cover with boiling water, and let stand for about 2 minutes, or until the skins start to split. Pour away the water. Peel the tomatoes, then halve them and scoop out the seeds with a teaspoon. Chop the flesh into small dice.

2 Using a mortar and pestle or the end of a rolling pin, crush the coriander seeds as finely as possible. Discard the stems from the herbs and finely chop the leaves.

3 Mix together the diced tomatoes, coriander seeds, herbs, garlic, lemon zest and juice, and oil with a little salt and black pepper in a bowl. Cover with plastic wrap and store in a cooler. Heat through over medium heat when ready to serve.

4 ripe tomatoes
½ teaspoon coriander seeds
large handful of fresh herbs, such as chervil, flat leaf parsley, tarragon, and chives
1 garlic clove, finely chopped
finely grated zest and juice of 1 lemon
½ cup olive oil
salt and black pepper

Serves 6
Prep time **5 minutes**
Cooking time **2 minutes**

LEMON & VODKA SAUCE

THIS SPICY SAUCE, ENLIVENED WITH CHILE AND VODKA, IS REALLY GOOD SERVED WITH FRESH LINGUINE OR VERMICELLI, TOPPED WITH TOASTED SLIVERED ALMONDS AND EXTRA THYME, IF DESIRED.

1 Pare thin strips of zest from the lemon, using a lemon zester or sharp knife. Squeeze 1 tablespoon lemon juice.

2 Heat the oil in a saucepan, add the lemon zest, garlic, chile, and thyme and sauté gently for 2-3 minutes, or until the ingredients start to brown.

3 Add the cream cheese to the saucepan and heat through until it softens to the consistency of pouring cream. Stir in the vodka, lemon juice, and a little salt and serve hot.

1 lemon
2 tablespoons olive oil
2 garlic cloves, thinly sliced
1 red chile, seeded and thinly sliced
2 teaspoons chopped thyme, plus a little extra to garnish
½ cup cream cheese
2 tablespoons vodka
salt

Serves **2**
Prep time **10 minutes**
Cooking time **5 minutes**

DILL & MUSTARD SAUCE

THIS SWEDISH SAUCE IS SWEET BUT TANGY AND STRONGLY FLAVORED WITH DILL. IT CAN BE MADE AHEAD AND KEEPS WELL IN A COOLER FOR A COUPLE OF DAYS. SERVE IT WITH HOT OR COLD SMOKED FISH, PARTICULARLY SALMON, OR WITH A WARM, NEW POTATO SALAD. LEFTOVERS ARE DELICIOUS WITH SALADS OR IN COLD MEAT SANDWICHES.

1 Pull the dill from the sprigs and chop finely. Put the mustards, sugar, and vinegar into a bowl and add a little salt.

2 Whisking constantly, gradually add the oil in a steady stream until the sauce is thick and smooth.

3 Stir in the dill, then taste and adjust the seasoning, adding a little more salt, vinegar or sugar, if desired.

large handful of dill
2 tablespoons mild
   whole-grain mustard
1 teaspoon Dijon mustard
2 tablespoons sugar
3 tablespoons white wine vinegar
$2/3$ cup olive oil
salt

Serves **8**
Prep time **10 minutes**

CAMPING TIP

Put a picnic or travel rug underneath your air bed or camping mat. This stops all the heat from disappearing directly into the ground and makes for a much cozier night under the stars.

**SWEET & SOUR SPICED
PINEAPPLE & MANGO**

**CHOCOLATE &
BANANA MELTS**

MULLED CRANBERRY & RED WINE

QUICK KIWI CHEESECAKES

SWEET STUFF & DRINKS

HOT BARBECUED
Fruit Salad

1 Cut off the top and bottom of the pineapple, using a sharp knife, then place it standing upright on a cutting board. Cut downward to remove the skin, working all around the pineapple. Cut the pineapple flesh into chunks. (In a small pineapple, the core is usually sweet and soft enough to eat, but if not, remove it before cutting into chunks.)

2 Peel the mango and slice the flesh away from the pit. Cook the mango and pineapple on a grill rack over a hot barbecue grill or campfire for 4 minutes on each side and the nectarine, peach, and apricots for 3 minutes on each side, until lightly charred. If you prefer, thread smaller fruit pieces onto metal skewers before cooking.

3 Serve the grilled fruit topped with Greek yogurt, drizzled with honey, and sprinkled with cardamom seeds, if using.

1 small pineapple
1 mango
1 nectarine, quartered and pitted
1 peach, quartered and pitted
2 apricots, halved, or quartered if large, and pitted
¼ cup Greek yogurt
honey, for drizzling
few cardamom seeds (optional)

Serves 4
Prep time 15 minutes
Cooking time 8 minutes

Fruit Salad KEBABS

• •

1 Put all the syrup ingredients and ½ cup water in a small saucepan and bring slowly to a boil, stirring occasionally, until the sugar has dissolved, then boil rapidly for 1 minute. Let cool slightly.

2 Cut the top and bottom off the pineapple, then cut away the skin. Cut into 8 wedges, cutting through the top down to the bottom. Remove the core, then thickly slice the wedges. Put the fruit into a shallow dish.

3 Quarter the papaya and scoop out the black seeds with a spoon. Peel away the skin, then thickly slice. Cut the peach into chunks and halve the strawberries. Mix all the fruits together in a bowl and pour the warm syrup over them. Cover with plastic wrap and let stand for 1 hour, or overnight, if preferred, to let the flavors develop.

4 Thread the fruit onto 8 metal skewers (or wooden skewers that have been soaked in cold water for 30 minutes) and cook on a grill rack over a hot barbecue grill or campfire for about 10 minutes, turning several times and brushing with the syrup, until hot and browned around the edges.

5 Serve the kebabs with spoonfuls of yogurt mixed with a little of the syrup, if desired.

½ large pineapple
1 papaya
1 peach, halved and pitted
8 large strawberries, hulled
Greek yogurt, to serve

Syrup
¼ teaspoon Chinese 5-spice powder
½ cup firmly packed light brown sugar
grated zest and juice of 1 lemon

Serves 4
Prep time **20 minutes, plus marinating**
Cooking time **15 minutes**

GRILLED PEACHES
WITH PASSION FRUIT

1 Cook the peach halves, cut side down, on a grill rack over a hot barbecue grill or campfire for 3-4 minutes, or until lightly charred. Turn the peaches over, drizzle with the honey and dust with cinnamon, then cook for another 2 minutes, or until softened.

2 Transfer to bowls and serve topped with Greek yogurt and the passion fruit pulp.

6 large ripe peaches, halved and pitted
2 tablespoons honey, plus extra to serve
2 teaspoons ground cinnamon

To serve
½ cup Greek yogurt
pulp from 2 passion fruit

Serves 4
Prep time **5 minutes**
Cooking time **about 5 minutes**

Creole
PINEAPPLE WEDGES

1 small pineapple
1 tablespoon dark rum
juice of 1 lime
1½ tablespoons sesame seeds

Serves 4
Prep time **10 minutes**
Cooking time **10 minutes**

1 Cut the pineapple lengthwise, first in half and then into quarters, leaving the leaves intact. The wedges should be about ½ inch thick, so it may be necessary to divide the quarters again.

2 Mix together the dark rum and lime juice in a bowl, then sprinkle the mixture over the pineapple slices.

3 Cook the pineapple on a grill rack over a hot barbecue grill or campfire for about 10 minutes, turning to be sure of even cooking. Serve sprinkled with sesame seeds.

CAMPING TIP

Solar-powered string lights not only make your tent look pretty but also act as a handy guide home when you're wandering back in the middle of the night, especially if you're on a busy site with a hundred identical tents.

MINI STRAWBERRY
Shortcakes

1 cup cream cheese
2 teaspoons confectioners' sugar
8 graham crackers or plain homemade cookies (see page 11)
4 teaspoons strawberry preserves
1²/₃ cups hulled and sliced strawberries

Serves 4
Prep time 20 minutes, plus chilling

1 Beat the cream cheese in a bowl to soften, then stir in the confectioners' sugar.

2 Spread a graham cracker or plain cookie with 1 teaspoon of the strawberry preserves, then spread one-quarter of the cream cheese mixture over the top. Lay a few strawberry slices on top of the cream cheese, then top with a second cracker or cookie. Repeat to make 3 more shortcakes.

3 Transfer to a plastic container with a lid and chill in a cooler for a least 1 hour before serving.

Boozy Blueberry &
MASCARPONE DESSERTS

1 Mix together three-quarters of the blueberries and the alcohol in a bowl, cover with plastic wrap, and let soak for at least 1 hour. Mash the blueberries.

2 Beat together the mascarpone and yogurt in a separate bowl until smooth, then mix in the sugar and lime zest and juice.

3 Layer alternate spoonfuls of mashed blueberries and mascarpone in bowls or glasses, top with the whole blueberries, and serve.

1½ cups blueberries
2 tablespoons kirsch or vodka
⅔ cup mascarpone cheese
⅔ cup plain yogurt
2 tablespoons sugar
grated zest and juice of 1 lime

....
Serves **4**
Prep time **15 minutes**,
plus soaking
....

CAMPING TIP

When they are available, campers always underestimate how many coins they need for coin-operated conveniences such as showers and clothes dryers, and coins will become like gold dust if your campsite charges for these or anything else for that matter!

SWEET & SOUR SPICED
Pineapple & Mango

1 firm, ripe mango
1 small pineapple, sliced in half
  lengthwise and then into thin
  wedges
2 tablespoons confectioners'
  sugar, plus extra to serve

Sweet and sour dressing
½ long red chile, seeded and
  finely chopped
¼ cup lime juice
2 tablespoons packed light
  brown sugar
1-2 tablespoons finely
  shredded mint

Serves 4
Prep time **10 minutes**
Cooking time **8 minutes**

1 Heat a ridged grill pan over medium-high heat.

2 Cut the mango into 2 pieces, using the pit as a guide and cutting either side of it. Sift confectioners' sugar all over the cut sides of the mango and pineapple so they are well covered.

3 Lay the mango, cut side down, and pineapple in the hot pan and grill for 2 minutes, rotating the pieces once so that a charred crisscross pattern appears on the fruit. Turn the pineapple wedges over and repeat on the other side. This may need to be done in two batches.

4 Meanwhile, to make the sweet and sour dressing, put the chile, lime juice, sugar, and mint into a small bowl, then stir until the sugar is dissolved. Set aside.

5 Transfer the fruits to plates and drizzle with the dressing. Serve dusted with extra confectioners' sugar, if desired.

PASSION FRUIT YOGURT WHIPS

1 cup heavy cream
6 passion fruit, halved, flesh
    and seeds removed
1¼ cups Greek yogurt
1 tablespoon honey
4 pieces of shortbread or
    homemade cookies (see
    page 11), to serve

Serves 4
Prep time 8 minutes

1 Whip the cream in a bowl until it forms soft peaks.

2 Put the passion fruit flesh and seeds, yogurt, and honey into a separate bowl and stir together, then fold in the cream.

3 Spoon into tall glasses or bowls and serve with the cookies.

FIGS WITH YOGURT & HONEY

• •

8 ripe figs
¼ cup plain yogurt
2 tablespoons honey

Serves 4
Prep time **5 minutes**
Cooking time **10 minutes**

1 Heat a ridged grill pan until hot. Slice the figs in half, then add to the pan, skin side down, and cook for 10 minutes, until the skins begin to blacken.

2 Serve the figs with spoonfuls of yogurt and some honey spooned over the top.

LEMON & PASSION FRUIT WHIPS

½ cup crushed shortbread
   cookies
⅔ cup heavy cream
½ cup lemon-flavor yogurt
2 passion fruit, halved

Serves **2**
Prep time **10 minutes**

1 Divide the crushed cookies between two glasses or bowls.
Whip the cream in a bowl until just thick enough to form soft
peaks, then lightly fold in the yogurt with the seeds and pulp
from 1 of the passion fruit.

2 Spoon the mixture into the glasses, spoon the remaining
passion fruit seeds and pulp over the top, and serve.

STEWED RHUBARB
with Vanilla Pudding

1 Put the rhubarb, orange juice or water, and ground ginger, if using, into a large saucepan. Add as much of the remaining sugar as you like, depending on sweetness desired, to the rhubarb. Heat until the sugar has dissolved, then simmer gently, stirring occasionally, for about 8 minutes, or until the rhubarb is tender. Remove from the heat and let cool slightly.

2 Spoon the rhubarb into bowls and spoon the vanilla pudding over the top to serve.

1½ lb rhubarb, cut into 1½ inch lengths (about 5 cups)
3 tablespoons orange juice or water
½ teaspoon ground ginger (optional)
¼–½ cup sugar
2 cups store-bought vanilla pudding

Serves **4-6**
Prep time **5 minutes**
Cooking time **15 minutes**

BLUEBERRY & ORANGE
Meringues

1 Put the vanilla pudding or custard, yogurt, orange zest, and vanilla bean paste or extract into a bowl and stir until well combined.

2 Put two-thirds of the blueberries in four glasses or bowls. Spoon the berries over the yogurt mixture, then top each glass with a lightly crushed meringue. Sprinkle with the remaining blueberries and serve immediately.

1 cup fresh vanilla pudding
  or custard
1 cup blueberry yogurt
1 teaspoon finely grated
  orange zest
1 teaspoon vanilla bean
  paste or extract
1 cup blueberries
4 store-bought meringues
  nests

Serves 4
Prep time 10 minutes

CINNAMON & RAISIN PEAR TRIFLE

1 Put the raisins, half of the cinnamon, and ½ cup of the juice from the pears in a saucepan over medium-high heat and bring to a gentle boil, then simmer over low heat for 1 minute. Turn off the heat and let stand for 5 minutes.

2 Beat the vanilla pudding or custard with the remaining cinnamon in a bowl and slice the pears into thick pieces.

3 Place the panettone in the bottom of four bowls. Pour the warm raisin mixture over the panettone cubes and cover with the sliced pears. Pour over the vanilla pudding or custard, cover with plastic wrap, and chill in a cooler for about 10 minutes.

4 Spoon 1 tablespoon of the crème fraîche or Greek yogurt over each trifle and serve sprinkled with the hazelnuts.

½ cup raisins
1 teaspoon cinnamon
1 (15 oz) can pears in juice
2 cups fresh vanilla pudding or custard
6 oz panettone, cut into bite-size cubes
¼ cup crème fraîche or Greek yogurt
½ cup roasted hazelnuts, coarsely chopped

Serves 4
Prep time **20 minutes, plus chilling**
Cooking time **5 minutes**

CHOCOLATE & BANANA MELTS

1 Place half the bread slices on a board and top each with the chocolate, banana, and marshmallows. Top with the remaining bread.

2 Brush the sandwiches lightly with oil and cook on a grill rack over a barbecue grill or campfire for 1-2 minutes. Flip the sandwiches over and cook for another 1-2 minutes, until golden.

8 slices of white bread, crusts removed
3 oz semisweet chocolate, finely chopped
1 large banana, sliced
8 marshmallows, chopped
vegetable oil, for brushing

Serves **4**
Prep time **5 minutes**
Cooking time **2-4 minutes**

COOKING TIP

If you're feeling really lazy, just make a slit in each banana skin, put a couple of squares of chocolate in, and grill until softened.

BLUEBERRY & GINGER
PATTIES

1 Put the flour and baking powder into a bowl, add the butter, and rub in with the fingertips until the mixture resembles fine bread crumbs. Stir in the ginger, blueberries, and sugar.

2 Add the milk to the bowl and mix with a blunt knife to make a soft dough. Turn out onto a lightly floured board and shape into a log. Cut across into 12 pieces, all roughly the same size and about ½ inch thick.

3 Heat a little oil in a skillet, add several of the patties, and cook until golden on the underside. Turn the patties over and cook for another few minutes, until golden and cooked through. Remove from the pan, lightly dust with sugar, and serve warm with yogurt.

4 Repeat with the remaining patties, adding a little more oil to the pan as required.

1⅔ cups all-purpose flour, plus extra for dusting
2½ teaspoons baking powder
4 tablespoons salted butter, cubed
2 pieces of preserved ginger, finely chopped
½ cup dried blueberries
2 tablespoons sugar, plus extra for dusting
⅓ cup milk
vegetable oil, for frying
Greek yogurt, to serve

Serves **4**
Prep time **20 minutes**
Cooking time **15-20 minutes**

S'mores

7 oz milk chocolate, broken into pieces
18 marshmallows
plenty of graham crackers or homemade cookies (see page 11)

Makes **about 18**
Prep time **20 minutes**
Cooking time **3 minutes**

1 Put the chocolate in a heatproof bowl and place on a grill rack over the coolest area of a barbecue grill or campfire.

2 Thread the marshmallows onto several metal skewers, leaving a space between each, then heat over the fire, turning them until lightly toasted.

3 For each s'more, spread a little melted chocolate onto a cracker or cookie, top with a toasted marshmallow and then another chocolate-coated cracker or cookie, and press together gently so the marshmallow spreads to form a filling.

CHOC CINNAMON
French Toast

2 eggs
2 thick slices of seeded whole
    wheat bread, cut in half
1 tablespoon butter
2 tablespoons sugar
2 teaspoons unsweetened
    cocoa powder
½ teaspoon ground cinnamon

Serves **2**
Prep time **2 minutes**
Cooking time **5 minutes**

1 Lightly beat the eggs in a shallow dish. Dip the bread slices in the mixture, turning them over so they've absorbed the batter on both sides.

2 Melt the butter in a skillet until foaming, add the egg-coated bread, and cook for about 5 minutes, turning occasionally, until golden on both sides.

3 Mix the sugar, cocoa powder, and cinnamon on a plate. Transfer the hot egg-coated bread to the plate and coat in the mixture. Serve immediately.

COOKING TIP

Serve with the glossy chocolate sauce on page 246 for a chocoholic's dream dish!

QUICK KIWI
& Ginger Cheesecakes

10 gingersnaps
½ cup cream cheese
⅓ cup crème fraîche or Greek
   yogurt
1 piece of preserved ginger,
   chopped
1 tablespoon syrup from the jar
   of preserved ginger
2 kiwis, peeled and sliced

Serves **4**
Prep time **10 minutes**

1 Put the gingersnaps into a plastic bag and crush them, using a rolling pin or other heavy item. Sprinkle the crushed cookies over the bottom of four glasses or bowls.

2 Beat the cream cheese, crème fraîche or yogurt, preserved ginger and syrup in a bowl, then spoon the mixture over the cookies. Arrange the kiwi slices on top of the cheesecakes and serve.

Glossy
CHOCOLATE SAUCE

1 Put the sugar and ½ cup of water into a small saucepan and cook over low heat, stirring constantly with a wooden spoon, until the sugar has completely dissolved.

2 Bring the syrup to a boil and boil for 1 minute, then remove the pan from the heat and let cool for 1 minute. Add the chocolate to the pan.

3 Add the butter and heat until the chocolate and butter have melted, stirring frequently, until the sauce is smooth and glossy. If the last of the chocolate doesn't melt completely or you want to serve the sauce warm, return the pan briefly to a low heat.

⅔ cup sugar
7 oz semisweet chocolate, chopped
2 tablespoons unsalted butter

Serves **4-6**
Prep time **5 minutes**
Cooking time **about 5 minutes**

Applesauce

4 tablespoons butter
3 large cooking apples, peeled, cored, and chopped
¼ cup sugar
6 whole cloves
finely grated zest and juice of 1 lemon
salt

Serves **6**
Prep time **10 minutes**
Cooking time **20 minutes**

1 Melt the butter in a saucepan and add the apples, sugar, cloves, lemon zest and juice, and a little salt. Cover with a lid and let cook gently over the lowest heat for about 20 minutes, stirring the mixture occasionally, until the apples are soft and mushy.

2 Adjust the seasoning, if necessary, adding a little more lemon juice for a tangier flavor, if desired. Transfer to a bowl and serve warm or cold.

MULLED CRANBERRY & RED WINE

1 (1 ¼ pint) bottle inexpensive
   red wine
2½ cups cranberry juice
½ cup (4 oz) brandy, rum,
   vodka, or orange liqueur
½ cup sugar
1 orange
8 cloves
1-2 cinnamon sticks (depending
   on size)

To serve
1 orange, cut into segments
2-3 bay leaves
few fresh cranberries

Makes **8-10 glasses**
Prep time **10 minutes**
Cooking time **10 minutes**

1 Pour the red wine, cranberry juice, and brandy or other
   alcohol into a large saucepan and stir in the sugar.

2 Stud the orange segments with a clove. Break the
   cinnamon sticks into large pieces and add to the pan with
the orange pieces. Cover with a lid and heat gently for about
10 minutes, until warm.

3 Replace the orange segments with fresh ones and add
   the bay leaves and cranberries. Ladle into heatproof
glasses or mugs, keeping back the fruits and herbs, if desired.

Frothy Hot Toddy
CHOCOLATE DRINK

1 teaspoon cornstarch
1¼ cups low-fat milk
1 teaspoon sugar
4 squares of semisweet
  chocolate
2 tablespoons alcohol of your
  choice, such as brandy, rum,
  or vodka
1 teaspoon grated chocolate
  (semisweet, milk, or white),
  to serve

1 Put the cornstarch into a bowl and mix in 1 tablespoon of the milk to make a smooth paste. Stir in scant 1 cup of the milk, the sugar, chocolate, and alcohol.

2 Pour into a saucepan and heat through until hot, then pour into a tall mug.

3 Heat the remaining milk and whisk vigorously. Pour over the hot chocolate, sprinkle with the grated chocolate, and serve immediately.

Serves **1**
Prep time **5 minutes**
Cooking time **5 minutes**

RUSTY NAIL

AN AFTER-DINNER DRINK THE NAME OF WHICH
IS PROBABLY BECAUSE OF ITS COLOR AND NOT
IMMIGRANT SCOTTISH BARTENDERS STIRRING THE
COCKTAIL WITH A RUSTY NAIL BEFORE SERVING IT
TO THEIR AMERICAN PATRONS, AS LEGEND HAS IT.

ice cubes, if available
1½ measures Scotch whisky
1 measure Drambuie

Serves 1
Prep time **3 minutes**

1 Fill a short glass with ice cubes, if using. Pour over the
whisky and Drambuie and serve.

Whisky MAC

A WARMING SLUG MADE WITH EQUAL MEASURES OF SCOTCH AND GINGER WINE,
THIS IS A DELICIOUS PICK-ME-UP.

3-4 ice cubes, if available
1 measure Scotch whisky
1 measure ginger wine

1 Put the ice cubes, if using, in a short glass. Pour over the
whisky and ginger wine, stir lightly, and serve.

Serves 1
Prep time **3 minutes**

Pimm's Cocktail

1 Fill a tall glass with ice, if using, then add the Pimm's.

2 Put the cucumber and fruit slices in the glass and top up with the lemon-flavor soda. Decorate with the mint sprig and serve.

ice cubes, if available
1 measure Pimm's No. 1
cucumber slices
1 strawberry
apple slices
lemon slices
orange slices
3 measures lemon-flavor soda
1 mint sprig, to garnish

Serves 1
Prep time 10 minutes

INDEX

ACKNOWLEDGMENTS

Picture Credits

Key: a above, b below, c center, l left, r right, bk background

CGTextures 32 bk (throughout), 47 bk (throughout), 149 bk (throughout), 163 bk; Jacobo Cortés Ferreira 20 bk (throughout). **Octopus Publishing Group** 25, 251; Craig Robertson; 12 br, 26; David Jordan 15; David Loftus 201; David Munns 181, 249; Gareth Sambridge 237; Ian Garlick 179 ar, 205; Ian Wallace 2 a, 12 al, 12 ar, 19, 27, 39 al, 39 b, 40, 43, 48, 49, 61, 68, 71, 73, 75, 77, 89, 93 c, 96, 122, 144, 152, 155, 165, 187, 226 ar, 230, 242; Lis Parsons 2 b, 2 c, 12 bl, 16, 21, 39 ar, 41, 55, 56, 57, 65, 72, 78, 85, 93 a, 95, 99, 105, 106, 107, 111, 143, 146 bl, 149, 161, 168, 169, 173, 175, 179 b, 184, 189, 191, 197, 226 al, 226 bl, 235, 238, 240, 241, 245; Sean Myers 228; Simon Smith 133, 137, Stephen Conroy 13, 33, 37, 51, 69, 81, 93 b, 101, 118, 119, 127, 128, 135, 146 al, 146 ar, 151, 153, 157, 179 al, 183, 193, 194, 217 b, 219, 220, 222, 224, 226, 236, 247; William Reavell 139, 167, 209, 213; William Shaw 53, 121, 126, 130, 136, 146 br, 158, 162, 177, 185, 195, 239. **Shutterstock** Anastasiia Sorokina 4 a; Andrew Helbig 6 a; Andrey_Kuzmin 178-179 bk; aodaodaodaod 2-3 bk (throughout); artfood 146-147 bk; bikeriderlondon 115 a; BrAt82 12-13 bk (throughout), 15 bk (throughout); CandyBox Images 114; cobraphotography 216; Cranach 43 bk (throughout); Dutourdumonde Photography 5 b; Dzinnik Darius 217 a; Fedorov Oleksiy 23 bk (throughout); Goodluz 115 b; Grischa Georgiew 5 a; Jason Patrick Ross 83 a; kao 1 bk (throughout); Kotenko Oleksandr 83 b; lightpoet 82; Loskutnikov 18 bk (throughout); magicinfoto 8 bk (throughout); mama_mia 29 l; mapraest 6 br; margouillat photo 125; Naffarts 6 bl; narinto 28-29 bk (throughout); Sander van der Werf 9; Svetlana Lukienko 28; Tanya Lomakivska 170; Triff 31 bk (throughout). **Thinkstock** donstock 29 b; EnginKorkmaz 6-7 bk (throughout); 60 bk (throughout); Fuse 171 b; loops7 14 bk (throughout); Madredus 30 bk (throughout); MKucova 171 a; ongap 3; Steve Mason 29 r; Oksana Lebedev 4-5 bk (throughout).

Publisher Sarah Ford
Editor Pauline Bache
Features Writer Cara Frost-Sharratt
Designers Eoghan O'Brien and Jaz Bahra
Picture Library Manager Jennifer Veall
Assistant Production Manager Lucy Carter

JUN - 2015